Y0-DBS-509

THE ROUND TABLE

This edition of "The Round Table" consists of one thousand copies printed from type.

THE ROUND TABLE

JAMES RUSSELL LOWELL

RICHARD G. BADGER
The Gorham Press
BOSTON

The Gorham Press, Boston, U. S. A.

CONTENTS

NATIONALITY IN LITERATURE

NATIONALITY IN LITERATURE [1]

TIME is figured with scythe, hour-glass, wallet, and slippery forelock. He is allegorized as the devourer of his own offspring. But there is yet one of his functions, and that not the least important, which wants its representative among his emblems. To complete his symbolical outfit, a sieve should be hung at his back. Busy as he must be at his mowing, he has leisure on his hands, scents out the treacherous saltpetre in the columns of Thebes, and throws a handful of dust over Nineveh, that the mighty hunter Nimrod may not, wanting due rites of sepulture, wander, a terrible shadow, on this side the irrepassable river. A figurative personage, one would say, with quite enough to do already, without imposing any other duty upon him. Yet it is clear that he finds opportunity also thoroughly to sift men and their deeds, winnowing away with the untired motion of his wings, monuments, cities, empires, families, generations, races, as chaff.

We must go to the middle of a child's bunch of cherries to be sure of finding perfect fruit. The outer circles will show unripened halves, stabs of

[1] *Kavanagh, a Tale.* By HENRY WADSWORTH LONGFELLOW. Boston: Ticknor, Reed & Fields. 1849.

the robin's bill, and rain-cracks, so soon does the ambition of quantity deaden the nice conscience of quality. Indeed, with all of us, men as well as children, amount passes for something of intrinsic value. But Time is more choice, and makes his sieve only the coarser from age to age. One book, one man, one action, shall often be all of a generation busy with sword, pen, and trowel, that has not slipped irrevocably through the ever-widening meshes.

We are apt to forget this. In looking at the literature of a nation, we take note only of such names as Dante, Shakspeare, Goethe, not remembering what new acres have been added to the wide chaff-desert of Oblivion, that we may have these great kernels free from hull and husk. We overlook the fact that contemporary literature has not yet been put into the sieve, and quite gratuitously blush for the literary shortcomings of a whole continent. For ourselves, we have long ago got rid of this national (we might call it hemispherical) sensitiveness, as if there were anything in our western half-world which stimulated it to produce great rivers, lakes, and mountains, mammoth pumpkins, Kentucky giants, two-headed calves, and what not, yet at the same time rendered it irremediably barren of great poets, painters, sculptors, musicians, and men generally. If there be any such system of natural compensations, whereby geological is balanced against human development, we may, at least, console ourselves with the anticipation, that America can never (from scientifically demonstrable inability) incur the odium of mothering the greatest fool.

There is, nevertheless, something agreeable in being able to shift the responsibility from our own shoulders to the broader ones of a continent. When anxious European friends inquire after our Art and our Literature, we have nothing to do but to refer them to Mount Washington or Lake Superior. It is their concern, not ours. We yield them without scruple to the mercies of foreign reviewers. Let those generously solicitous persons lay on and spare not. There are no such traitors as the natural features of a country which betray their sacred trusts. They should be held strictly to their responsibilities, as, in truth, what spectacle more shameful than that of a huge, lubberly mountain, hiding its talent under a napkin, or a repudiating river? Our geographers should look to it, and instil proper notions on this head. In stating the heights of our mountains and the lengths of our rivers, they should take care to graduate the scale of reproach with a scrupulous regard to every additional foot and mile. They should say, for example, that such a peak is six thousand three hundred feet high, and has never yet produced a poet; that the river so-and-so is a thousand miles long, and has wasted its energies in the manufacture of alligators and flatboatmen. On the other hand, they should remember to the credit of the Mississippi, that, being the longest river in the world, it has very properly produced the longest painter, whose single work would overlap by a mile or two the pictures of all the old masters stitched together. We can only hope that it will never give birth to a poet long in proportion.

Since it seems to be so generally conceded, that the form of an author's work is entirely determined by the shape of his skull, and that in turn by the peculiar configuration of his native territory, perhaps a new system of criticism should be framed in accordance with these new developments of science. Want of sublimity would be inexcusable in a native of the mountains, and sameness in one from a diversified region, while flatness could not fairly be objected to a dweller on the prairies, nor could eminent originality be demanded of a writer bred where the surface of the country was only hilly or moderately uneven. Authors, instead of putting upon their titlepages the names of previous works, or of learned societies to which they chance to belong, should supply us with an exact topographical survey of their native districts. The Himalaya mountains are, we believe, the highest yet discovered, and possibly society would find its account in sending the greater part of our poets thither, as to a university, either by subscription or by a tax laid for the purpose. How our literature is likely to be affected by the acquisition of the mountain ranges of California, remains to be seen. Legislators should certainly take such matters into consideration in settling boundary lines, and the General Court of Massachusetts should weigh well the responsibility it may incur to posterity, before transferring to New York the lofty nook of Boston Corner with its potential Homers and Miltons.

But perhaps we have too hastily taken the delinquency of our physical developments for granted. Nothing has hitherto been demanded of rivers and lakes in other parts of the world, except fish and mill privileges, or, at most, a fine waterfall or a pretty island. The received treatises on mountainous obstetrics give no hint of any parturition to be expected, except of mice. So monstrous a conception as that of a poet is nowhere on record; and what chloroform can we suggest to the practitioner who should be taken unawares by such a phenomenon?

At least, before definite sentence be passed against us, the period of gestation which a country must go through, ere it bring forth a great poet, should be ascertained with scientific exactness. Let us not be in any hurry to resort to a Cesarian operation. Poets, however valuable in their own esteem, are not, after all, the most important productions of a nation. If we can frame a commonwealth in which it shall not be a misfortune to be born, in which there shall never be a pair of hands nor a mouth too much, we shall be as usefully employed as if we should flower with a Dante or so, and remain a bony stalk forever after. We can, in the meantime, borrow a great poet when we want one, unless the pleasure and profit which we derive from the works of a great master, depend upon the proprietary right in him secured to us by compatriotism. For ourselves, we should be strongly inclined to question any exclusive claim to Shakspeare on the part of our respected relative, John Bull, who could do nothing better than look foolish when the great dramatist was called *bizarre,* and who has never had either the taste or the courage to see a single one of his most characteristic plays acted as he wrote it.

The feeling that it was absolutely necessary to our respectability that we should have a literature, has been a material injury to such as we have had. Our criticism has oscillated between the two extremes of depreciation and overpraise. On the one hand, it has not allowed for the variations of the magnetic needle of taste, and on the other, it has estimated merit by the number of degrees west from Greenwich. It seems never to have occurred to either sect of critics, that there were such things as principles of judgment immutable as those of mathematics. One party has been afraid to commend lest an English Reviewer might afterward laugh; the other has eulogized because it considered so terrible a catastrophe probable. The Stamp Act and the Boston Port Bill scarcely produced a greater excitement in America than the appalling question, *Who reads an American book?* It is perfectly true, that the amount of enlightenment which a reader will receive from a book depends upon the breadth of surface which he brings within its influence, for we never get *something* for *nothing;* but we would deferentially suggest for the relief of many a still trembling soul, repeating to itself the *quid sum miser tunc dicturus* to that awful question from the Edinburgh judgment-seat, that it is barely possible that the *power* of a book resides in the book itself, and that real books somehow compel an audience without extraneous intervention. From the first, it was impossible that Art should show here the successive stages of growth which have characterized it in the Old World. It is only geographically that we can call ourselves a new nation. However else our literature may avoid the payment of its liabilities, it can surely never be by a plea of infancy. Intellectually, we were full-grown at the start. Shakspeare had been dead five years, and Milton was eleven years old, when Mary Chilton leaped ashore on Plymouth Rock.

In looking backward or forward mentally, we seem to be infected with a Chinese incapacity of perspective. We forget the natural foreshortening, taking objects as they are reflected upon our retina, and neglecting to supply the proper interstices of time. This is equally true whether we are haruspicating the growth of desired opinions and arts, or are contemplating those which are already historical. Thus, we know statistically the amount which any race or nation has stored in its intellectual granaries, but make no account of the years of scarcity, of downright famine even, which have intervened between every full harvest. There is an analogy between the successive stages of a literature and those of a plant. There is, first of all, the seed, then the stalk, and then the seed again. What a length of stalk between Chaucer and Spenser, and again between Milton and Wordsworth! Except in India, perhaps, it would be impossible to affirm confidently an indigenous literature. The seed has been imported, accidentally or otherwise, as the white-weed and Hessian fly into America. Difference of soil, climate, and exposure will have their legitimate influence, but characteristics enough ordinarily remain for the tracing of the pedigree. The locality of its original production is as indisputable as that of the garden of Eden. Only this is certain, that our search carries us farther and farther eastward.

No literature, of which we have authentic record or remains, can be called national in this limited and restricted sense. Nor, if one could be found, would the calling it so be commendation. The best parts of the best authors in all languages can be translated; but, had they this element of exclusive nationality, the idea would demand a lexicon as well as the language which enveloped it. This shell within a shell would give more trouble in the cracking than any author can safely demand of his readers. Only a Dante can compel us to take an interest in the petty local politics of his day. No grubs were ever preserved in such amber. No Smiths and Browns were ever elevated upon so sublime and time-defying pinnacles of love, horror, and pity. The key by which we unlock the great galleries of Art is their common human interest. Nature supplies us with lexicon, commentary, and glossary to the great poems of all ages.

It would be hard to estimate the immediate indebtedness of Grecian literature; easier to reckon how much must have been due to the indirect influence of a religion and philosophy, whose esoteric ideas were of Egyptian derivation. Aristophanes is perhaps the only Grecian poet who is characterized by that quality of nationality of which we are speaking. Nay, it is something intenser than mere nationality in which his comedy is steeped. It is not the spirit of Greece, not even of Attica, but of Athens. It is cockneyism, not nationality. But his humor is more than Athenian. Were it not so, it would be dreary work enough deciphering jokes, as it were, in a mummypit, by the dim light of the scholiast's taper, too choked with dust and smoke to do anything but cough when we are solemnly assured that we have come to the point.

There is a confusion in men's minds upon this subject. Nationality and locality are not distinguished from one another; and were this jumble fairly cleared up, it would appear that there was a still farther confounding of truth to nature with fidelity of local coloring. Mere nationality is no more nor less than so much provincialism, and will be found but a treacherous antiseptic for any poem. It is because they are men and women, that we are interested in the characters of Homer. The squabbles of a score of petty barbarian chiefs, and the siege of a city which never existed,[2] would

[2] Written before Schliemann's discoveries.—Ed.

have been as barren and fruitless to us as a Welsh genealogy, had the foundations of the Iliad been laid no wider and deeper than the Troad. In truth, the only literature which can be called purely national is the Egyptian. What poetry, what philosophy, the torch of the Arab has fruitlessly lighted up for European eyes, we as yet know not; but that any ideas valuable to mankind are buried there, we do not believe. These are not at the mercy of sand, or earthquake, or overflow. No race perishes without intellectual heirs, but whatever was locally peculiar in their literature, their art, or their religious symbols, becomes in time hieroglyphical to the rest of the world, to be, perhaps, painfully deciphered for the verification of useless history, but incapable of giving an impulse to productive thought. Literature survives, not because of its nationality, but in spite of it.

After the United States had achieved their independence, it was forthwith decided that they could not properly be a nation without a literature of their own. As if we had been without one! As if Shakspeare, sprung from the race and the class which colonized New England, had not been also ours! As if we had no share in the puritan and republican Milton, we who had cherished in secret for more than a century the idea of the great puritan effort, and at last embodied it in a living commonwealth! But this ownership in common was not enough for us, and, as partition was out of the question, we must have a drama and an epos of our own. It must be national, too; we must have it all to ourselves. Other nations kept their poets, and so must we. We were to set up a literature as people set up a carriage, in order to be as good as our neighbors. It was even seriously proposed to have a new language. Why not, since we could afford it? Beside, the existing ones were all too small to contain our literature whenever we should get it. One enthusiast suggested the ancient Hebrew, another a firenew tongue of his own invention. Meanwhile, we were busy growing a literature. We watered so freely, and sheltered so carefully, as to make a soil too damp and shaded for anything but mushrooms; wondered a little why no oaks came up, and ended by voting the mushroom an oak, an American variety. Joel Barlow made the lowest bid for the construction of our epos, got the contract, and delivered in due season the Columbiad, concerning which we can only regret that it had not been entitled to a still higher praise of nationality by being written in one of the proposed new languages.

One would think that the Barlow experiment should have been enough. But we are still requested by critics, both native and foreign, to produce a national literature, as if it were some school exercise in composition to be handed in by a certain day. The sharp struggle of a day or a year may settle the question of a nation's political independence, but even for that, there must be a long moral preparation. The first furrow drawn by an English plow in the thin soil of Plymouth was truly the first line in our Declaration of Independence. Jefferson was not the prophet looking forth into the future, but the scribe sitting at the feet of the past. But nationality is not a thing to be won by the sword. We may safely trust to the influence of our institutions to produce all of it that is valuable. Let us be content that, if we have been to blame for a Columbiad, we have also given form, life, and the opportunity of entire development to social ideas ever reacting with more and more force upon the thought and the literature of the Old World.

The poetry and romance of other nations are assumed to be national, inasmuch as they occupy themselves about local traditions or objects. But we, who never had any proper youth as a nation, never had our mythic period either. We had no cradle and no nursery to be haunted with such bugaboos. One great element of external and immediate influence is therefore wanting to our poets. They cannot, as did Goethe in his "Faust," imbue an old legend, which already has a hold upon the fancy and early associations of their countrymen, with a modern and philosophical meaning which shall make it interesting to their mature understandings and cultivated imaginations. Whatever be the cause, no race into whose composition so large a Teutonic element has entered, is divided by such an impassable chasm of oblivion and unbelief from the ancestral mythology as the English. Their poets accordingly are not popular in any true sense of the word, and have influenced the thought and action of their countrymen less than those of any other nation except those of ancient Rome. Poets in other countries have mainly contributed to the creating and keeping alive of national sentiment; but the English owe theirs wholly to the sea which islands them. Chaucer and Spenser are Normans, and their minds open most fairly southward. Skelton, the Swift of his day, a purely English poet, is forgotten. Shakspeare, thoroughly English as he is, has chosen foreign subjects for the greatest of his dramas, as if to show that genius is cosmopolitan. The first thorough study, criticism, and consequent appreciation of him we owe to the Germans; and he can in no sense be called national except by accident of birth. Even if we grant that he drew his fairy mythology from any then living faith among his countrymen, this formed no bond of union between him and them, and was even regarded as an uncouthness and barbarism till long after every vestige of such faith was obliterated. If we concede any nationality to Milton's great poem, we must at the same time allow to the English an exclusive title to the localities where the scene is laid, a title which they would hardly be anxious to put forward in respect, at least, to one of them. When he was meditating a national poem, it was, he tells us, on the legend of Arthur, who, if he had ever existed at all, would have been English only in the same sense that Tecumseh is American. Coleridge, among his thousand reveries, hovered over the same theme, but settled at last upon the siege of Jerusalem by Titus as the best epical subject remaining. Byron, in his greatest poem, alludes only to England in a rather contemptuous farewell. Those strains of Wordsworth, which have entitled his name to a place on the selecter list of English poets, are precisely the ones in which England has only a common property with the rest of mankind. He could never have swum over Lethe with the sonnets to the river Duddon in his pocket. Whether we look for the cause in the origin of the people, or in their insular position, the English mind has always been characterized by an emigrating tendency. Their most truly national epic was the colonizing of America.

If we admit that it is meritorious in an author to seek for a subject in the superstitions, legends, and historical events of his own peculiar country or district, yet these (unless delocalized by their own intrinsic meaning) are by nature ephemeral, and a wide tract of intervening years makes them as truly foreign as oceans, mountains, or deserts could. Distance of time passes its silent statute of outlawry and alienage against them, as effectually as distance of space. Indeed, in that strictness with which the martinets of nationality use the term, it would be a hard thing for any people to prove an exclusive title to its myths and legends. Take, for example, the story of Wayland the Smith, curious as furnishing the undoubted original of the incident of Tell and the apple, and for its analogies with the Grecian fable of Dædalus. This, after being tracked through the *folklore* of nearly all the nations of Northern Europe, was at last, to the great relief of the archæologic mind, supposed to be *treed* in Scandinavia, because the word *voelund* was found to mean smith among the Icelanders. Yet even here we cannot rest secure that this piece of mythical property has been restored to its rightful owners. As usual in such cases, investigation points Asia-ward, and the same word is found with the same signification in Ceylon. However unsatisfying in other respects, the search has at least turned up a euphonious synonym for the name Smith, which might be assumed by any member of that numerous patronymic guild desirous of attaining a nearer approach to individuality.

But even the most indisputable proof of original ownership is of no great account in these matters. These tools of fancy cannot be branded with the name of any exclusive proprietor. They are his who can use them. Poor Peter Claus cries out in vain that he has been robbed of himself by the native of a country undiscovered when he took his half-century's nap on the Kypphauser mountains. *Caret vate sacro,* and nobody gives him the least heed. He has become the shadow, and Rip Van Winkle the substance. Perhaps he has made up his mind to it by this time, and contrives to turn an honest penny among the shades by exhibiting himself as the *Original* Rip Van Winkle. We trust, for the honor of our country, that Rip brazens it out there, and denounces the foreign impostor in the purest—American, we were going to say; but here another nationality interposes its claim, and we must put up with Low Dutch.

The only element of permanence which belongs to myth, legend, or history, is exactly so much of each as refuses to be circumscribed by provincial boundaries. Whence once superstitions, customs, and historic personages are dead and buried in antiquarian treatises or county annals, there is no such thing as resurrection for them. The poet who encumbers himself with them takes just that amount of unnecessary burthen upon his shoulders. He is an antiquary, not a creator, and is writing what posterity will read as a catalogue rather than a poem. There is a homeliness about great genius which leads it to glorify the place of its "kindly engendure," (as Chaucer calls it,) either by a tender allusion, or by images and descriptions drawn from that fairest landscape in the gallery of memory. But it is a strange confusion of thought to attribute to a spot of earth the inspiration whose source is in a universal sentiment. It is the fine humanity, the muscular sense, and the generous humor of Burns which save him from being merely Scotch, like a score of rhymesters as national as he. The Homers of Little Pedlington die, as their works died before them, and are forgotten; but let a genius get born there, and one touch of his nature shall establish even for Little Pedlington an immortal consanguinity which the whole world shall be eager to claim. The field-mouse and the mountain-daisy are not Scotch, and Tam o' Shanter died the other day within a mile of where we are writing. Measuring Burns by that which is best in him, and which ensures to him a length of life coincident with that of the human heart, he is as little national as Shakspeare, and no more an alien in Iowa than in Ayrshire. There is a vast difference between truth to nature and truth to fact; an impassable gulf between genius, which deals only with the true, and that imitative faculty which patiently and exactly reproduces the actual. This makes the distinction between the works of Fielding, which delight and instruct forever, and those of Smollett, which are of value as affording a clear insight into contemporaneous modes of life, but neither warm the heart nor impregnate the imagination. It is this higher and nobler kind of truth which is said to characterize the portraits of Titian, which gives an indefinable attraction to those of Page, and which inspires the busts of Powers. This excuses meagreness of color and incorrectness of drawing in Hogarth, who was truly rather a great dramatist than a great painter, and gives them that something which even indifferent engraving cannot destroy, any more than bad printing can extinguish Shakspeare.

This demand for a nationality bounded historically and geographically by the independent existence and territory of a particular race or fraction of a race, would debar us of our rightful share in the past and the ideal. It was happily illustrated by that parochially national Gascon, who would have been edified by the sermon had it been his good fortune to belong to the parish. Let us be thankful that there is no court by which we can be excluded from our share in the inheritance of the great poets of all ages and countries, to which our simple humanity entitles us. No great poet has ever sung but the whole human race has been, sooner or later, the wiser and better for it. Above all, let us not tolerate in our criticism a principle which would operate as a prohibitory tariff of ideas. The intellect is a diœcious plant, and books are the bees which carry the quickening pollen from one to another mind. It detracts nothing from Chaucer that we can trace in him the influences of Dante and Boccaccio; nothing from Spenser that he calls Chaucer master; nothing from Shakspeare that he acknowledges how dear Spenser was to him; nothing from Milton that he brought fire from Hebrew and Greek altars. There is no degradation in such indebtedness. Venerable rather is this apostolic succession, and inspiring to see the *vitai lampada* passed thus from consecrated hand to hand.

Nationality, then, is only a less narrow form of provincialism, a sublimer sort of clownishness and ill-manners. It deals in jokes, anecdotes, and allusions of such purely local character that a majority of the company are shut out from all approach to an understanding of them. Yet so universal a demand must have for its basis a more or less solid substratum of truth. There are undoubtedly national, as truly as family, idiosyncrasies, though we think that these will get displayed without any special schooling for that end. The substances with which a nation is compelled to work will modify its results, as well intellectual as material. The still renewing struggle with the unstable desert sands gave to the idea of durability in the Egyptian imagination a preponderance still further increased by the necessity of using granite, whose toughness of fibre and vagueness of coloring yielded unwillingly to fineness of outline, but seemed the natural helpmates of massiveness and repose. The out-of-door life of the Greeks, conducing at once to health and an unconscious education of the eye, and the perfection of physical development resulting from their palæstral exercises and constantly displayed in them, made the Greeks the first to perceive the noble symmetry of the human figure, for embodying the highest types of which Pentelicus supplied the fittest material. Corporeal beauty and strength, therefore, entered largely into their idea of the heroic, and perhaps it was rather policy than dandyism which hindered Alcibiades from learning to play the flute. With us, on the other hand, clothed to the chin in the least graceful costume ever invented by man, and baked half the year with stoves and furnaces, beauty of person has gradually receded from view, and wealth or brain is the essential of the modern novelist's hero. It may not be fanciful to seek in climate, and its resultant effects upon art, the remote cause of that fate-element which entered so largely into the Greek drama. In proportion as sculpture became more perfect, the images of the gods became less and less merely symbolical, and at last presented to the popular mind nothing more than actual representations of an idealized humanity. Before this degradation had taken place, and the divinities had been vulgarized in marble to the common eye, the ideas of the unseen and supernatural came to the assistance of the poet in giving interest to the struggles or connivances between heroes and gods. But presently a new and deeper chord of the imagination must be touched, and the unembodiable shadow of Destiny was summoned up, to move awe and pity as long as the human mind is incapable of familiarizing by precise definition the fearful and the vague. In that more purely objective age, the conflict must be with something external, and the struggles of the mind with itself afforded no sufficient theme for the poet. With us introspection has become a disease, and a poem is a self-dissection.

That Art in America will be modified by circumstances, we have no doubt, though it is impossible to predict the precise form of the moulds into which it will run. New conditions of life will stimulate thought and give new forms to its expression. It may not be our destiny to produce a great literature, as, indeed, our genius seems to find its kindliest development in practicalizing simpler and more perfect forms of social organization. We have yet many problems of this kind to work out, and a continent to subdue with the plough and the railroad, before we are at leisure for æsthetics. Our spirit of adventure will first take a material and practical direction, but will gradually be forced to seek outlet and scope in unoccupied territories of the intellect. In the meantime we may fairly demand of our literature that it should be national to the extent of being as free from outworn conventionalities, and as thoroughly impregnated with humane and manly sentiment, as is the idea on which our political fabric rests. Let it give a true reflection of our social, political, and household life. The "Poems on Man in the Republic," by Cornelius Mathews, disfigured as they were by gross faults of dialect and metre, had the great merit of presenting the prominent features of our civilization in an American light. The story of "Margaret" is the most emphatically *American* book ever written. The want of plan and slovenliness of construction are characteristic of a new country. The scenery, character, dialect, and incidents mirror New England life as truly as Fresh Pond reflects the sky. The moral, also, pointing forward to a new social order, is the intellectual antitype of that restlessness of disposition, and facility of migration which are among our chief idiosyncrasies. The mistake of our imaginative writers generally is that, though they may take an American subject, they *costume* it in a foreign or antique fashion. The consequence is a painful vagueness and unreality. It is like putting Roman drapery upon a statue of Washington, the absurdity of which does not strike us so forcibly because we are accustomed to it, but which we should recognize at once were the same treatment applied to Franklin. The old masters did exactly the reverse of this. They took ancient or foreign subjects, but selected their models from their own immediate neighborhood. When Shakspeare conceived his Athenian mechanics, he did not cram with Grecian antiquities in order to make them real in speech and manners. Their unconscious prototypes were doubtless walking Stratford streets, and demonstrating to any one who had clear enough eyes, that stupidity and conceit were precisely the same things on the banks of the Avon and those of the Ilissus. Here we arrive at the truth which is wrapped up and concealed in the demand for nationality in literature. It is neither more nor less than this, that authors should use their own eyes and ears, and not those of other people. We ask of them human nature as it appears in man, not in books; and scenery not at second hand from the canvas of painter or poet, but from that unmatched landscape painted by the Great Master upon the retina of their own eyes. Though a poet should make the bobolink sing in Attica, the *anachorism* is nothing, provided he can only make it truly sing so that we can hear it. He will have no difficulty in making his peace with posterity. The error of our advocates of nationality lies in their assigning geographical limits to the poet's range of historical characters as well as to his natural scenery. There is no time or place in human nature, and Prometheus, Coriolanus, Tasso, and Tell are ours if we can use them, as truly as Washington or Daniel Boone. Let an American author make a living character, even if it be antediluvian, and nationality will take care of itself. The newspaper, the railroad, and the steamship are fast obliterating the externals of distinct and hostile nationality. The Turkish soldier has shrunk into coat and pantaloons, and reads Dickens. But human nature is everywhere the same, and everywhere inextinguishable. If we only insist that our authors shall be good, we may cease to feel nervous about their being national. Excellence is an alien nowhere. And even if, as we hear it lamented, we have no literature, there are a thousand other ways of making ourselves useful. If the bobolink and mockingbird find no poet to sing them, they can afford, like Kepler, to wait; and in the meantime they themselves will sing as if nothing had happened. For ourselves, we confess, we have hopes. The breed of poets is not extinct, nor has Apollo shot away all the golden, singing arrows in his quiver. We have a very strong persuasion, amounting even to faith, that eyes and ears will yet open on this Western Continent, and find adequate utterance. If some of our birds have a right to feel neglected, yet other parts of our natural history have met with due civility; and if the pine tree complain of the tribute which Emerson has paid it, we surrender it to the lumberer and the saw-mill without remorse. It must be an unreasonable tree, wooden at head and heart.

Nay, how are we to know what is preparing for

us at this very moment? What herald had Chaucer, singing the matins of that grand cathedral-service whose vespers we have not yet heard, in England? What external circumstance controlled the sweet influence of Spenser? Was Gorboduc a prologue that should have led us to expect Hamlet? Did the Restoration furnish the score for those organ-strains of Milton, breaking in with a somewhat unexpected voluntary to drown the thin song of pander and parasite with its sublime thunders of fervor and ascription? What collyrium of nationality was it that enabled those pleasant Irish eyes of Goldsmith to pierce through the artificial tinsel and frippery of his day to that little clump of roses at Wakefield? England had long been little better than a province of France in song, when Wordsworth struck the note of independence, and led the people back to the old worship. While we are waiting for our literature, let us console ourselves with the following observation with which Dr. Newman commences his History of the Hebrew Monarchy. "Few nations," he says, "which have put forth a wide and enduring influence upon others, proclaim themselves to have been indigenous on the land of their celebrity." Or, if the worst come, we can steal a literature like the Romans, and thus acquire another point of similarity to that remarkable people, whom we resemble so much, according to the Quarterly Review, in our origin.

Mr. Longfellow has very good-naturedly and pointedly satirized the rigid sticklers for nationality in one of the chapters of his "Kavanagh," which we have taken for the text of some remarks we have long intended to make on this subject. It is time that we should say something about the book itself. But before doing this, we wish to clear a few misconceptions which seem to stand in the way of its fair appreciation.

It is quite too common a practice, both with readers and the more superficial class of critics, to judge a book by what it is *not,* a matter much easier to determine than what it *is.* Not only has the public taste lost its tone by constant and long-continued literary opium-eating, and indulgence in romances highly spiced with adventure, passion, and crime, but the faculty of judgment (the bile which secretes the nutritive portion of our intellectual food) has become weakened and indecisive under the everlasting flood of romantic slops with which we daily dilute it. People also very frequently take the last book they have read by an admired author as the standard by which to measure the next that comes in their way, no matter how dissimilar in artistic treatment and intention. Or they merely ask the question, does it interest *me?* and thus make their private taste (or want of it) a criterion of merit, when it should rightfully only decide the question whether they shall read it or let it alone. In such cases, the old English form of expression would be both safe and modest, and *it likes me* or *it likes me not* would perhaps express more precisely the true state of the affair.

The first question to be asked is, what was the author's intention? Then, how has he fulfilled it? "Kavanagh," one may say pretty confidently, is *not* a novel, nor a romance, nor a drama. It is neither exciting, nor thrilling, nor harrowing, nor tempestuously passionate, nor gloomily terrible, nor—in short it is not nonsense, it is "Kavanagh." We waive for the present the question whether it be a fault that it is not what the author especially meant that it should not be. That is a grave difficulty, and one well demanding the intervention of a Scriblerus. *Too nun-like for me,* says Public Taste, looking at the lily of the valley; *pity it is not a rose!* Then, turning to the rose, *an open-bosomed thing, the Nell Gwynne of flowers,—ah, if it were only a lily of the valley!* For ourselves, we are willing to be thankful for both, as long as nature is bountiful enough to give them.

The word, "Tale," upon the title-page, if it be not merely a formal suffix, like the "*Esq.*" in the address of all American letters, we consider a misnomer. We think a truer name for the book would be, a prose pastoral. It had been better to have called it "Kavanagh" simply, and left it to the reader to find out what it was. And it is not as reader, but as critic, that we make the complaint. For, if we look at it critically as assuming this specific character, we find it wanting in many particulars. Where the chief concern is completeness of narrative effect, there should be no loose ends. Every divergent thread and fibre must be taken up and twisted firmly into the compact strand of the leading design. If we hold "Kavanagh" strictly to its responsibilities as a "Tale," we shall be obliged to condemn in it a disproportion of parts to the whole, and an elaboration of particulars at the expense of unity. The truth is, that there are two distinct interests in "Kavanagh," one, that of the *story,* which centres in Alice, the other, that of the *moral,* which is illustrated wholly by Churchill. Now Churchill is made too prominent as respects any relation he has to the *tale,* while the *moral* is weakened by his knowing nothing of the breaking of Alice's heart, nor, indeed, of her love. As an instance of what we mean by the disproportion spoken of above, we should cite the whole scene between Churchill and Mr. Hathaway, which, though true to the life, is false to the interests of the story. So of some of the conversations between Churchill and his wife; they do not carry forward the plot, nor add to our insight into his character. Even if they did, they would be too large in proportion to the rest, though we should not willingly give up the Hindoo Mathematics. It seems to us, that if some chapters of the book had been given as leaves from Churchill's diary, and he made acquainted with the double passion for Kavanagh, the parts would have been in better keeping, and the force of the moral heightened.

We are glad to dissociate our twofold character of reader and critic, to which the fate of the Dioscuri sometimes may happen, the one being in life and light, while the other is in the shades. Let us see if we cannot find some condition on which they may enjoy sunshine and happiness together. As readers, we, in common with the rest, have only thanks to offer. All who love purity of tone, tenderness, and picturesque simplicity, have incurred a new obligation to the author of "Kavanagh." We will now look at it in what we consider its truer character of pastoral. In this kind of composition, repose is the leading characteristic. A tender pensiveness of tone best fulfils here the requisites of art. It allows of humor and pathos, only both must be subdued, and neither grief nor merriment must be allowed so noisy a vent as would jar upon the ear soothed by a certain out-of-doors quiet and contentment. It is a story told to us, as it were, while we lie under a tree, and the ear is willing at the same time to take in other sounds. The gurgle of the brook, the rustle of the leaves, even noises of life and toil (if they be distant,) such as the rattle of the white-topped wagon and the regular pulse of the thresher's flail, reconcile themselves to the main theme, and reinforce it with a harmonious accompaniment. In "Kavanagh" as in "Evangeline," we conceive it to be a peculiar merit that the *story* is kept down with so rigid a self-denial. The brass of the orchestra is not allowed an undue prominence. This perfect keeping, this unanimity, so to speak, was more striking in "Evangeline" than in the present work. The author is here and there tempted out of his way, and allows his hobby-horse to leap the fences of proportion. For example, the division numbered thirteen has no manner of business in the book. We feel it as an unwarrantable intrusion, and do not at once recover our composure. It affects the interest and attention, as an ill-matching of the figure on two breadths of carpet affects the eye, which is conscious of it even when turned the other way. We were going to object to the episode of Sally Manchester, as having no necessary connection with the rest of the story, and as not tending in any way to advance the plot. But we remember that the design here does not make the several parts subservient to the main incident. This is not so much a narrative as a succession of scenes. We walk through the streets of the village with a friend who is giving, as we go along, a sketch of the touching drama which has passed under the unconscious eyes of Churchill in search of a plot. As we saunter on, we have glimpses of an interior, now and then, through open door or window, and our friend interrupts himself to tell us who that was that passed, or to parenthesize a good story about the person on the other side of the street to whom he himself directs our attention. There is no want of harmony in the variety, and we retract our half-uttered criticism, the more readily as we consider the letter of Mr. Cherryfield as one of the best things in the book. It is absolutely perfect.

"Kavanagh" is, as far as it goes, an exact daguerreotype of New England life. We say *daguerreotype,* because we are conscious of a certain absence of motion and color, which detracts somewhat from the vivacity, though not from the truth, of the representation. From Mr. Pendexter with his horse and chaise, to Miss Manchester painting the front of her house, the figures are faithfully after nature. The story, too, is remarkably sweet and touching. The two friends, with their carrier-dove correspondence, give us a pretty glimpse into the trans-boarding-school disposition of the maiden mind, which will contrive to carry everyday life to romance, since romance will not come to it. The accident by which Alice discovers Kavanagh's love for Cecilia is a singularly beautiful invention; but we should wish to see with our own eyes before we believed that a king*fisher* ever pursued a dove, or, indeed, anything but a fish. Even the king*bird,* which does carry on a guerilla warfare with crows and hawks (slow-flighted birds,) would hardly pursue a pigeon, the swiftest of all flyers.

It is not unusual to make a single work the opportunity for passing definitive judgment upon an author. This is not our view of the duty of a critic. He is limited to the book before him, and all departures from it are impertinences. We hope that Mr. Longfellow may live a great many years yet, and give us a great many more books. We shall not undertake to pass a sentence which he may compel us to revise. We shall only say that he is the most popular of American poets, and that this popularity may safely be assumed to contain in itself the elements of permanence, since it has been fairly earned, without any of that subservience to the baser tastes of the public which characterizes the quack of letters. His are laurels honorably gained and gently worn. Without comparing him with others, it is enough if we declare our conviction, that he has composed poems which will live as long as the language in which they are written.

THOREAU'S "A WEEK ON THE CONCORD AND MERRIMACK RIVERS"

THOREAU'S "A WEEK ON THE CONCORD AND MERRIMACK RIVERS"[1]

WE stick to the sea-serpent. Not that he is found in Concord or Merrimack, but like the old Scandinavian snake, he binds together for us the two hemispheres of Past and Present, of Belief and Science. He is the link which knits us seaboard Yankees with our Norse progenitors, interpreting between the age of the dragon and that of the railroad-train. We have made ducks and drakes of that large estate of wonder and delight bequeathed to us by ancestral irkings, and this alone remains to us unthrift heirs of Linn. We give up the Kraken, more reluctantly the mermaid, for we once saw one, no *mulier formosa, supernè,* no green-haired maid with looking-glass and comb, but an adroit compound of monkey and codfish, sufficiently attractive for purposes of exhibition till the suture where the *desinit in piscem* began, grew too obtrusively visible.

We feel an undefined respect for a man who has seen the sea-serpent. He is to his brother-fishers what the poet is to his fellow-men. Where they have seen nothing better than a school of horse-mackerel, or the idle coils of ocean around Half-

[1] *A Week on the Concord and Merrimack Rivers.* By HENRY D. THOREAU. Boston and Cambridge: James Monroe & Company. 1849.

way Rock, he has caught authentic glimpses of the withdrawing mantlehem of the Edda-age. We care not for the monster himself. It is not the thing, but the belief in the thing, that is dear to us. May it be long before Professor Owen is comforted with the sight of his unfleshed vertebræ, long before they stretch many a rood behind Kimball's or Barnum's glass, reflected in the shallow orbs of Mr. and Mrs. Public, which stare but see not! When we read that Captain Spalding of the pinkstern *Three Pollies* has beheld him rushing through the brine like an infinite series of bewitched mackerel-casks, we feel that the mystery of old Ocean, at least, has not yet been sounded, that Faith and Awe survive there unevaporate. We once ventured the horsemackerel theory to an old fisherman, browner than a tomcod. "Hosmackril!" he exclaimed indignantly, "hosmackril be—" (here he used a phrase commonly indicated in laical literature by the same sign which serves for Doctorate in Divinity,) "don't yer spose *I* know a hosmackril?" The intonation of that *"I"* would have silenced Professor Monkbairns Owen with his provoking *phoca* forever. What if one should ask *him* if he knew a trilobite?

The fault of modern travelers is that they see nothing out of sight. They talk of eocene periods and tertiary formations, and tell us how the world looked to the plesiosaur. They take science (or nescience) with them, instead of that soul of generous trust their elders had. All their senses are skeptics and doubters, materialists reporting things for other skeptics to doubt still further upon. Nature becomes a reluctant witness upon the stand, badgered with geologist hammers and phials of acid. There have been no travelers since those included in Hakluyt and Purchas, except Martin, perhaps, who saw an inch or two into the invisible at the Orkneys. We have peripatetic lecturers, but no more travelers. Travelers' stories are no longer proverbial. We have picked nearly every apple (wormy or otherwise,) from the world's tree of Knowledge, and that without an Eve to tempt us. Two or three have hitherto hung luckily beyond reach on a lofty bough shadowing the interior of Africa, but there is a Doctor Bialloblotzky at this very moment pelting at them with sticks and stones. It may be only next week, and these, too, bitten by geographers and geologists, will be thrown away. We wish no harm to this worthy Sclavonian, but his name is irresistibly suggestive of boiled lobster, and some of the natives are not so choice in their animal food.

Analysis is carried into everything. Even Deity is subjected to chemic tests. We must have exact knowledge, a cabinet stuck full of facts pressed, dried, or preserved in spirits, instead of a large, vague world our fathers had. Our modern Eden is a *hortus siccus*. Tourists defraud rather than enrich us. They have not that sense of æsthetic proportion which characterized the elder traveler. Earth is no longer the fine work of art it was, for nothing is left to the imagination. Job

Hortop, arrived at the height of the Bermudas, thinks it full time to throw us in a merman,—"we discovered a monster in the sea who showed himself three times unto us from the middle upwards, in which parts he was proportioned like a man, of the complection of a mulatto or tawny Italian." Sir John Hawkins is not satisfied with telling us about the merely sensual Canaries, but is generous enough to throw us in a handful over: "About these islands are certain flitting islands, which have been oftentimes seen, and when men approached near them they vanished, . . . and therefore it would seem he is not yet born to whom God hath appointed the finding of them." Henry Hawkes describes the visible Mexican cities, and then is not so frugal but that he can give us a few invisible ones. "The Spaniards have notice of seven cities which the old men of the Indians show them should lie toward the N. W. from Mexico. They have used, and use daily, much diligence in seeking of them, but they cannot find any one of them." Thus do these generous ancient mariners make children of us again. Their successors show us an earth effete and past bearing, tracing out with the eyes of industrious fleas every wrinkle and crowfoot.

The journals of the elder navigators are Prose Odysseys. The geographies of our ancestors were works of fancy and imagination. They read poems where we yawn over items. Their world was a huge wonder-horn, exhaustless as that which Thor strove to drain. Ours would scarce quench the small thirst of a bee. No modern voyager brings back the magical foundation stones of a Tempest. No Marco Polo, traversing the desert beyond the city of Lok, would tell of things able to inspire the mind of Milton with

> "Calling shapes and beckoning shadows dire
> And airy tongues that syllable men's names
> On sands and shores and desert wildernesses."

It was easy enough to believe the story of Dante, when two-thirds of even the upper-world were yet untraversed and unmapped. With every step of the recent traveler our inheritance of the wonderful is diminished. Those beautifully pictured notes of the Possible are redeemed at a ruinous discount in the hard and cumbrous coin of the actual. How are we not defrauded and impoverished? Does California vie with El Dorado, or are Bruce's Abyssinian Kings a set-off for Prester John? A bird in the bush is worth two in the hand. And if the philosophers have not even yet been able to agree whether the world has any existence independent of ourselves, how do we not gain a loss in every addition to the catalogue of Vulgar Errors? Where are the fishes which nidificated in trees? Where the monopodes sheltering themselves from the sun beneath their single umbrella-like foot, umbrella-like in everything but the fatal necessity of being borrowed? Where the Acephali, with whom Herodotus, in a kind of ecstasy, wound up his climax of men with abnormal top-pieces? Where the Roc whose eggs are possibly boulders, needing no far-fetched theory of glacier or iceberg to account for them? Where the tails of the Britons? Where the no legs of the bird of Paradise? Where the Unicorn with that single horn of his, sovereign against all manner of poisons? Where the fountain of Youth? Where that Thessalian spring which, without cost to the county, convicted and punished perjurers? Where the Amazons of Orellana? All these, and a thousand other varieties we have lost, and have got nothing instead of them. And those who have robbed us of them have stolen that which not enriches themselves. It is so much wealth cast into the sea beyond all approach of diving bells. We owe no thanks to Mr. J. E. Worcester, whose Geography we studied enforcedly at school. Yet even he had his relentings, and in some softer moment vouchsafed us a fine, inspiring print of the Maelstrom, answerable to the twenty-four mile diameter of its suction. Year by year, more and more of the world gets disenchanted. Even the icy privacy of the arctic and antarctic circles is invaded. Our youth are no longer ingenious, as indeed no ingenuity is demanded of them. Everything is accounted for, everything cut and dried, and the world may be put together as easily as the fragments of a dissected map. The Mysterious bounds nothing now on the North, South, East, or West. We have played Jack Horner with our earth, till there is never a plum left in it.

Since we cannot have back the old class of voyagers, the next thing we can do is to send poets out a-travelling. These will at least see all that remains to be seen, and in the way it ought to be seen. These will disentangle nature for us from the various snarls of man, and show us the mighty mother without paint or padding, still fresh and young, full-breasted, strong-backed, fit to suckle and carry her children. The poet is he who bears the charm of freshness in his eyes. He may safely visit Niagara, or those adopted children of nature the Pyramids, sure to find them and to leave them as if no eye had vulgarized them before. For the ordinary tourist all wells have been muddied by the caravans that have passed that way, and his eye, crawling over the monuments of nature and art, adds only its quota of staleness.

Walton quotes an "ingenious Spaniard" as saying, that "rivers and the inhabitants of the watery element were made for wise men to contemplate and fools to pass by without consideration," and Blount, in one of the notes to his translation of Philostratus, asserts that "as travelling does much advantage wise men, so does it no less prejudice fools." Mr. Thoreau is clearly the man we want. He is both wise man and poet. A graduate of Cambridge—the fields and woods, the axe, the hoe, and the rake have since admitted him *ad eundem*. Mark how his imaginative sympathy goes beneath the crust, deeper down than that of Burns, and needs no plough to turn up the object of its muse. "It is pleasant to think in winter, as we walk over the snowy pastures, of those happy dreamers that lie under the sod, of dormice and all that race of dormant creatures which have such a superfluity of life enveloped in thick folds of fur, impervious to the cold." "For every oak and birch, too, growing on the hilltop, as well as for these elms and willows, we knew that there was a graceful, ethereal and ideal tree making down from the roots, and sometimes nature in high tides brings her mirror to its foot and makes it visible." Only some word were better here than *mirror* (which is true to the fact, but not to the fancy,) since we could not see *through* that. Leigh Hunt represents a colloquy between man and fish, in which both maintain their orthodoxy so rigidly that neither is able to comprehend or tolerate the other. Mr. Thoreau flounders in no such shallows. He is wiser, or his memory is better, and can re-create the sensations of that part of his embryonic life which he passed as a fish. We know nothing more thoroughly charming than his description of twilight at the river's bottom.

"The light gradually forsook the deep water, as well as the deeper air, and the gloaming came to the fishes as well as to us, and more dim and gloomy to them, whose day is perpetual twilight, though sufficiently bright for their weak and watery eyes. Vespers had already rung in many a dim and watery chapel down below, where the shadows of the weeds were extended in length over the sandy floor. The vespertinal pout had already begun to flit on leathern fin, and the finny gossips withdrew from the fluvial streets to creeks and coves, and other private haunts, excepting a few of stronger fin, which anchored in the stream, stemming the tide even in their dreams. Meanwhile, like a dark evening cloud, we were wafted over the cope of their sky, deepening the shadows on their deluged fields."

One would say this was the work of some bream Homer. Melville's pictures of life in Typee have no attraction beside it. Truly we could don scales, pectorals, dorsals, and anals, (critics are already cold-blooded,) to stroll with our dumb love, fin in fin, through the Rialto of this subfluvial Venice. The Complete Angler, indeed! Walton had but an extraqueous and coquine intimacy with the fishes compared with this. His tench and dace are but the poor transported convicts of the frying-pan.

There was a time when Musketaquid and Merrimack flowed down from the Unknown. The adventurer wist not what fair reaches stretched before him, or what new dusky peoples the next bend would discover. Surveyor and map have done what they could to rob them of their charm of unexpectedness. The urns of the old river-gods have been twitched from under their arms and set up on the museum-shelf, or, worse yet, they serve to boil the manufacturer's plum-porridge. But Mr. Thoreau with the touch of his oar conjures back as much as may be of the old enchantment. His map extends to the bed of the river, and he makes excursions into finland, penetrating among the scaly tribes without an angle. He is the true cosmopolitan or citizen of the Beautiful. He is thoroughly impartial—*Tros, Tyriusve*—a lichen or a man, it is all one, he looks on both with equal eyes. We are at a loss where to class him. He might be Mr.

Bird, Mr. Fish, Mr. Rivers, Mr. Brook, Mr. Wood, Mr. Stone, or Mr. Flower, as well as Mr. Thoreau. His work has this additional argument for freshness, the birds, beasts, fishes, trees, and plants having this advantage, that none has hitherto gone among them in the missionary line. They are trapped for their furs, shot and speared for their flesh, hewn for their timber, and grubbed for Indian Vegetable Pills, but they remain yet happily unconverted in primitive heathendom. They take neither rum nor gunpowder in the natural way, and pay tithes without being Judaized. Mr. Thoreau goes among them neither as hunter nor propagandist. He makes a few advances to them in the way of Boodhism, but gives no list of catechumens, though flowers would seem to be the natural followers of that prophet.

In truth, Mr. Thoreau himself might absorb the forces of the entire alphabetic sanctity of the A.B.C.F.M., persisting as he does in a fine, intelligent paganism. We need no more go to the underworld to converse with shadows of old philosophers. Here we have the Academy brought to our doors, and our modern world criticised from beneath the shelter of the Portico. Were we writing commendatory verses after the old style, to be prefixed to this volume, we should begin somewhat thus:—

"If the ancient, mystique, antifabian
Was (so he claimed) of them that Troy town wan
Before he was born; even so his soul we see
(Time's ocean underpast) revive in thee,

> As, diving nigh to Elis, Arethuse
> Comes up to loose her zone by Syracuse."

The great charm of Mr. Thoreau's book seems to be, that its being a book at all is a happy fortuity. The door of the portfolio-cage has been left open, and the thoughts have flown out of themselves. The paper and types are only accidents. The page is confidential like a diary. Pepys is not more minute, more pleasantly unconscious. It is like a book dug up, that has no date to assign it a special contemporaneousness, and no name of author. It has been written with no uncomfortable sense of a public looking over the shoulder. And the author is the least ingredient in it, too. All which I saw and part of which I was, would be an apt motto for the better portions of the volume: a part, moreover, just as the river, the trees, and the fishes are. Generally he holds a very smooth mirror up to nature, and if, now and then, he shows us his own features in the glass, when we had rather look at something else, it is as a piece of nature, and we must forgive him if he allow it a too usurping position in the landscape. He looks at the country sometimes (as painters advise) through the triumphal arch of his own legs, and, though the upside-downness of the prospect has its own charm of unassuetude, the arch itself is not the most graceful.

So far of the manner of the book, now of the book itself. It professes to be the journal of a week on Concord and Merrimack Rivers. We must have our libraries enlarged, if Mr. Thoreau intend to complete his autobiography on this scale —four hundred and thirteen pages to a sennight! He begins honestly enough as the Boswell of Musketaquid and Merrimack. It was a fine subject and a new one. We are curious to know somewhat of the private and interior life of two such prominent and oldest inhabitants. Musketaquid saw the tremulous match half-doubtingly touched to the revolutionary train. The blood of Captain Lincoln and his drummer must have dribbled through the loose planks of the bridge for Musketaquid to carry down to Merrimack, that he in turn might mingle it with the sea. Merrimack is a drudge now, grinding for the Philistines, who takes repeated dammings without resentment, and walks in no procession for higher wages. But its waters remember the Redman, and before the Redman. They knew the first mammoth as a calf, and him a mere *parvenu* and modern. Even to the saurians they could say—we remember your grandfather.

Much information and entertainment were to be pumped out of individuals like these, and the pump does not *suck* in Mr. Thoreau's hands. As long as he continues an honest Boswell, his book is delightful, but sometimes he serves his two rivers as Hazlitt did Northcote, and makes them run Thoreau or Emerson, or, indeed, anything but their own transparent element. What, for instance, have Concord or Merrimack to do with Boodh, themselves professors of an elder and to them wholly sufficient religion, namely, the willing subjects of watery laws, to seek their ocean? We have digressions on Boodh, on Anacreon, (with translations hardly so good as Cowley,) on Persius, on Friendship, and we know not what. We come upon them like snags, jolting us headforemost out of our places as we are rowing placidly up stream or drifting down. Mr. Thoreau becomes so absorbed in these discussions, that he seems, as it were, to *catch a crab,* and disappears uncomfortably from his seat at the bow-oar. We could forgive them all, especially that on Books, and that on Friendship, (which is worthy of one who has so long commerced with Nature and with Emerson,) we could welcome them all, were they put by themselves at the end of the book. But as it is, they are out of proportion and out of place, and mar our Merrimacking dreadfully. We were bid to a river-party, not to be preached at. They thrust themselves obtrusively out of the narrative, like those quarries of red glass which the Bowery dandies (emulous of Sisyphus) push laboriously before them as breast-pins.

Before we get through the book, we begin to feel as if the author had used the term week, as the Jews did the number *forty,* for an indefinable measure of time. It is quite evident that we have something more than a transcript of his fluviatile experiences. The leaves of his portfolio and river-journal seem to have been shuffled together with a trustful dependence on some overruling printer-providence. We trace the lines of successive deposits as plainly as on the sides of a deep cut, or rather on those of a trench carried through made-land in the city, where choiceness of material has been of less import than suitableness to fill up, and where plaster and broken bricks from old buildings, oyster-shells, and dock mud have been shot pellmell together. Yet we must allow that Mr. Thoreau's materials are precious, too. His plaster has bits of ancient symbols painted on it, his bricks are stamped with mystic sentences, his shells are of pearl-oysters, and his mud from the Sacramento.

"Give me a sentence," prays Mr. Thoreau bravely, "which no intelligence can understand!" —and we think that the kind gods have nodded. There are some of his utterances which have foiled us, and we belong to that class of beings which he thus reproachfully stigmatizes as intelligences. We think it must be this taste that makes him so fond of the Hindoo philosophy, which would seem admirably suited to men, if men were only oysters. Or is it merely because, as he naïvely confesses in another place, "his soul is of a bright invisible *green?*" We would recommend to Mr. Thoreau some of the Welsh sacred poetry. Many of the Triads hold an infinite deal of nothing, especially after the bottoms have been knocked out of them by translation. But it seems ungrateful to find fault with a book which has given us so much pleasure. We have eaten salt (Attic, too,) with Mr. Thoreau. It is the hospitality and not the fare which carries a benediction with it, and it is a sort of ill breeding to report any oddity in the viands. His feast is here and there a little savage, (indeed, he professes himself a kind of volunteer Redman,) and we must make out with the fruits, merely giving a sidelong glance at the baked dog and pickled missionary, and leaving them in grateful silence.

We wish the General Court had been wise enough to have appointed our author to make the report on the Ichthyology of Massachusetts. Then, indeed, would the people of the state have known something of their aquicolal fellow-citizens. Mr. Thoreau handles them as if he loved them, as old Izaak recommends us to do with a worm in impaling it. He is the very Asmodeus of their private life. He unroofs their dwellings and makes us familiar with their loves and sorrows. He seems to suffer a sea-change, like the Scotch peasant who was carried down among the seals in the capacity of family physician. He balances himself with them under the domestic lily-pad, takes a family-bite with them, is made the confidant of their courtships, and is an honored guest at the wedding-feast. He has doubtless seen a pickerel crossed in love, a perch Othello, a bream the victim of an unappreciated idiosyncrasy, or a minnow with a mission. He goes far to convince us of what we have before suspected, that the fishes are the highest of organizations. The natives of that more solid atmosphere, they are not subject to wind or rain, they have been guilty of no Promethean rape, they have bitten no apple. They build no fences, holding their watery inheritance undivided. Beyond all other living things they mind their own business. They have not degenerated to the necessity of reform, swallowing no social pills, but living quietly on each other in a true primitive community. They are vexed with no theories of the currency which go deeper than the Newfoundland Banks. *Nimium fortunati!* We wish Mr. Thoreau would undertake a report upon them as a private enterprise. It would be the most delightful book of natural history extant.

Mr. Thoreau's volume is the more pleasant that with all its fresh smell of the woods, it is yet the work of a bookish man. We not only hear the laugh of the flicker, and the watchman's rattle of the red squirrel, but the voices of poets and philosophers, old and new. There is no more reason why an author should reflect trees and mountains than books, which, if they are in any sense real, are as good parts of nature as any other kind of growth. We confess that there is a certain charm for us even about a fool who has read myriads of books. There is an undefinable atmosphere around him, as of distant lands around a great traveler, and of distant years around very old men. But we think that Mr. Thoreau sometimes makes a bad use of his books. Better things can be got out of Herbert and Vaughan and Donne than the art of making bad verses. There is no harm in good writing, nor do wisdom and philosophy prefer crambo. Mr. Thoreau never learned bad rhyming of the river and the sky. He is the more culpable as he has shown that he can write poetry at once melodious and distinct, with rare delicacy of thought and feeling.

"My life is like a stroll upon the beach,
As near the ocean's edge as I can go,
My tardy steps its waves sometimes o'erreach,
Sometimes I stay to let them overflow.

"My sole employment 't is, and scrupulous care,
To place my gains beyond the reach of tides,
Each smoother pebble, and each shell more rare,
Which ocean kindly to my hand confides.

"I have but few companions on the shore,
They scorn the strand who sail upon the sea,
Yet oft I think the ocean they've sailed o'er
Is deeper known upon the strand to me.

"The middle sea contains no crimson dulse,
Its deeper waves cast up no pearls to view,
Along the shore my hand is on its pulse,
And I converse with many a shipwrecked crew."

If Mr. Emerson choose to leave some hard nuts for posterity to crack, he can perhaps afford it as well as any. We counsel Mr. Thoreau, in his own words, to take his hat and come out of that. If he prefer to put peas in his shoes when he makes private poetical excursions, it is nobody's affair. But if the public are to go along with him, they will find some way to boil theirs.

We think that Mr. Thoreau, like most solitary men, exaggerates the importance of his own thoughts. The "I" occasionally stretches up tall as Pompey's pillar over a somewhat flat and sandy expanse. But this has its counterbalancing advantage, that it leads him to secure many a fancy and feeling which would flit by most men unnoticed. The little confidences of nature which pass his neighbors as the news slips through the grasp of birds perched upon the telegraphic wires, he receives as they were personal messages from a mistress. Yet the book is not solely excellent as a Talbotype of natural scenery. It abounds in fine thoughts, and there is many a critical *obiter dictum* which is good law, as what he says of Raleigh's style.

"Sir Walter Raleigh might well be studied if only for the excellence of his style, for he is remarkable in the midst of so many masters. There is a natural emphasis in his style, like a man's tread, and a breathing space between the sentences, which the best of modern writing does not furnish. His chapters are like English parks, or say rather like a western forest, where the larger growth keeps down the underwood, and one may ride on horseback through the openings."

Since we have found fault with some of what we may be allowed to call the worsification, we should say that the prose work is done conscientiously and neatly. The style is compact and the language has an antique purity like wine grown colorless with age. There are passages of a genial humor interspersed at fit intervals, and we close our article with one of them by way of grace. It is a sketch which would have delighted Lamb.

"I can just remember an old brown-coated man who was the Walton of this stream, who had come over from Newcastle, England, with his son, the latter a stout and hearty man who had lifted an anchor in his day. A straight old man he was who took his way in silence through the meadows, having passed the period of communication with his fellows; his old experienced coat hanging long and straight and brown as the yellow pine bark, glittering with so much smothered sunlight, if you stood near enough, no work of art but naturalized at length. I often discovered him unexpectedly amid the pads and the gray willows when he moved, fishing in some old country method,—for youth and age then went a fishing together,—full of incommunicable thoughts, perchance about his own Tyne and Northumberland. He was always to be seen in serene afternoons haunting the river, and almost rustling with the sedge; so many sunny hours in an old man's life, entrapping silly fish, almost grown to be the sun's familiar; what need had he of hat or raiment any, having served out his time, and seen through such thin disguises? I have seen how his coeval fates rewarded him with the yellow perch, and yet I thought his luck was not in proportion to his years; and I have seen when, with slow steps and weighed down with aged thoughts, he disappeared with his fish under his low-roofed house on the skirts of the village. I think nobody else saw him; nobody else remembers him now, for he soon after died, and migrated to new Tyne streams. His fishing was not a sport, nor solely a means of subsistence, but a sort of solemn sacrament and withdrawal from the world, just as the aged read their bibles."

"ELSIE VENNER"

"ELSIE VENNER"[1]

ENGLISH literature numbers among its more or less distinguished authors a goodly number of physicians. Sir Thomas Browne was, perhaps, the last of the great writers of English prose whose mind and style were impregnated with imagination. He wrote poetry without meaning it, as many of his brother doctors have meant to write poetry without doing it, in the classic style of

"Inoculation, heavenly maid, descend!"

Garth's "Dispensary" was long ago as fairly buried as any of his patients; and Armstrong's "Health" enjoys the dreary immortality of being preserved in the collections, like one of those queer things they show you in a glass jar at the anatomical museums. Arbuthnot, a truly genial humorist, has hardly had justice done him. People laugh over his fun in the "Memoirs of Scriblerus," and are commonly satisfied to think it Pope's. Smollett insured his literary life in "Humphrey Clinker"; and we suppose his Continuation of Hume is still one of the pills which ingenuous youth is expected to gulp before it is strong enough to resist. Goldsmith's fame has steadily gained; and so has that of Keats, whom we may also fairly reckon in our list, though he remained

[1] *Elsie Venner.* A Romance of Destiny. By OLIVER WENDELL HOLMES. 2 vols. Boston: Ticknor & Fields. 1861.

harmless, having never taken a degree. On the whole, the proportion of doctors who have positively succeeded in our literature is a large one, and we have now another very marked and beautiful case in Dr. Holmes. Since Arbuthnot, the profession has produced no such wit; since Goldsmith, no author so successful.

Five years ago[2] it would have been only Dr. Holmes's intimate friends that would have considered the remarkable success he has achieved not only possible, but probable. They knew, that, if the fitting opportunity should only come, he would soon show how much stuff he had in him,—sterner stuff, too, than the world had supposed,—stuff not merely to show off the iris of a brilliant reputation, but to block out into the foundations of an enduring fame. It seems an odd thing to say that Dr. Holmes had suffered by having given proof of too much wit; but it is undoubtedly true. People in general have a great respect for those who scare them or make them cry, but are apt to weigh lightly one who amuses them. They like to be tickled, but they would hardly take the advice of their tickler on any question they thought serious. We have our doubts whether the majority of those who make up what is called "the world" are fond of wit. It rather puts them out, as Nature did Fuseli. They look on its crinkling play as men do at lightning; and while they grant it is very fine, are teased with an uncomfortable wonder as to where it is going to strike next. They would

[2] Written in 1861.—Ed.

rather, on the whole, it were farther off. They like well-established jokes, the fine old smoked-herring sort, such as the clown offers them in the circus, warranted never to spoil, if only kept dry enough. Your fresh wit demands a little thought, perhaps, or at least a kind of negative wit, in the recipient. It is an active meddlesome quality, forever putting things in unexpected and somewhat startling relations to each other; and such new relations are as unwelcome to the ordinary mind as poor relations to a *nouveau riche.* Who wants to be all the time painfully conceiving of the antipodes walking like flies on the ceiling? Yet wit is related to some of the profoundest qualities of the intellect. It is the reasoning faculty acting *per saltum,* the sense of analogy brought to a focus; it is generalization in a flash, logic by the electric telegraph, the sense of likeness in unlikeness, that lies at the root of all discoveries; it is the prose imagination, common-sense at fourth proof. All this is no reason why the world should like it, however; and we fancy that the question, *Ridentem dicere verum quid vetat?* was plaintively put in the primitive tongue by one of the world's gray fathers to another without producing the slightest conviction. Of course, there must be some reason for this suspicion of wit, as there is for most of the world's deep-rooted prejudices. There is a kind of surface-wit that is commonly the sign of a light and shallow nature. It becomes habitual *persiflage,* incapable of taking a deliberate and serious view of anything, or of conceiving the solemnities that environ life. This has made men distrustful of all laughers; and they are apt to confound in one sweeping condemnation with this that humor whose base is seriousness, and which is generally the rebound of the mind from over-sad contemplation. They do not see that the same qualities that make Shakspeare the greatest of tragic poets make him also the deepest of humorists.

Dr. Holmes was already an author of more than a quarter of a century's standing, and was looked on by most people as an *amusing* writer merely. He protested playfully and pointedly against this, once or twice; but, as he could not help being witty, whether he would or no, his audience laughed and took the protest as part of the joke. He felt that he was worth a great deal more than he was vulgarly rated at, and perhaps chafed a little; but his opportunity had not come. With the first number of the "Atlantic" it came at last, and wonderfully he profited by it. The public were first delighted, and then astonished. So much wit, wisdom, pathos, and universal Catharine-wheeling of fun and fancy was unexampled. "Why, good gracious," cried Madam Grundy, "we've got a *genius* among us at last! I always knew what it would come to!" "Got a fiddlestick!" says Mr. G.; "it's only rockets." And there was no little watching and waiting for the sticks to come down. We are afraid that many a respectable skeptic has a crick in his neck by this time; for we are of opinion that these are a new kind of rocket, that go without sticks, and *stay up* against all laws of gravity.

We expected a great deal from Dr. Holmes; we thought he had in him the makings of the best magazinist in the country; but we honestly confess we were astonished. We remembered the proverb, " 'Tis the pace that kills," and could scarce believe that such a two-forty gait could be kept up through a twelvemonth. Such wind and bottom were unprecedented. But this was Eclipse [1] himself; and he came in as fresh as a May morning, ready at a month's end for another year's run. And it was not merely the perennial vivacity, the fun shading down to seriousness, and the seriousness up to fun, in perpetual and charming vicissitude;—here was the man of culture, of scientific training, the man who had thought as well as felt, and who had fixed purposes and sacred convictions. No, the Eclipse-comparison is too trifling. This was a stout ship under press of canvas; and however the phosphorescent star-foam of wit and fancy, crowding up under her bows or gliding away in subdued flashes of sentiment in her wake, may draw the eye, yet she has an errand of duty; she carries a precious freight, she steers by the stars, and all her seemingly wanton zigzags bring her nearer to port.

When children have made up their minds to like some friend of the family, they commonly besiege him for a story. The same demand is made by the public of authors, and accordingly it was made of Dr. Holmes. The odds were heavy

[1] A famous race-horse at the time this article was written.—Ed.

against him; but here again he triumphed. Like a good Bostonian, he took for his heroine a *schoolma'am,* the Puritan Pallas Athene of the American Athens, and made her so lovely that everybody was looking about for a schoolmistress to despair after. Generally, the best work in imaginative literature is done before forty; but Dr. Holmes should seem not to have found what a Mariposa grant Nature had made him till after fifty.

There is no need of our analyzing "Elsie Venner," for all our readers know it as well as we do. But we cannot help saying that Dr. Holmes has struck a new vein of New-England romance. The story is really a romance, and the character of the heroine has in it an element of mystery; yet the materials are gathered from every-day New-England life, and that weird borderland between science and speculation where psychology and physiology exercise mixed jurisdiction, and which rims New England as it does all other lands. The character of Elsie is exceptional, but not purely ideal, like Christabel and Lamia. In Doctor Kittredge and his "hired man," and in the Principal of the "Apollinean Institoot," Dr. Holmes has shown his ability to draw those typical characters that represent the higher and lower grades of average human nature; and in calling his work a Romance he quietly justifies himself for mingling other elements in the composition of Elsie and her cousin. Apart from the merit of the book as a story, it is full of wit, and of sound thought sometimes hiding behind a mask of humor. Admirably conceived are the two clergymen, gradually changing sides almost without knowing it, and having that persuasion of consistency which men always feel, because they must always bring their creed into some sort of agreement with their dispositions.

There is something melancholy in the fact, that, the moment Dr. Holmes showed that he felt a deep interest in the great questions which concern this world and the next, and proved not only that he believed in something, but thought his belief worth standing up for, the cry of *Infidel* should have been raised against him by people who believe in nothing but an authorized version of Truth, they themselves being the censors. For our own part, we do not like the smell of Smithfield, whether it be Catholic or Protestant that is burning there; though, fortunately, one can afford to smile at the Inquisition, so long as its Acts of Faith are confined to the corners of sectarian newspapers. But Dr. Holmes can well afford to possess his soul in patience. The Unitarian John Milton has won and kept quite a respectable place in literature, though he was once forced to say, bitterly, that "new Presbyter was only old Priest writ large." One can say nowadays, *E pur si muove,* with more comfort than Galileo could; the world does move forward, and we see no great chance for any ingenious fellow-citizen to make his fortune by a "Yankee Heretic-Baker," as there might have been two centuries ago.

Dr. Holmes has proved his title to be a wit in the earlier and higher sense of the word, when it meant a man of genius, a player upon thoughts rather than words. The variety, freshness, and strength which he has lent to the pages of the "Atlantic Monthly" during the last three years seem to demand of us that we should add our expression of admiration to that which his countrymen have been so eager and unanimous in rendering.

"THE MARBLE FAUN"

"THE MARBLE FAUN"

IT is, we believe, more than thirty years since Mr. Hawthorne's first appearance as an author; it is twenty-three since he gave his first collection of "Twice-told Tales" to the world. His works have received that surest warranty of genius and originality in the widening of their appreciation downward from a small circle of refined admirers and critics, till it embraced the whole community of readers. With just enough encouragement to confirm his faith in his own powers, those powers had time to ripen and toughen themselves before the gales of popularity could twist them from the balance of a healthy and normal development. Happy the author whose earliest works are read and understood by the lustre thrown back upon them from his latest! For then we receive the impression of continuity and cumulation of power, of peculiarity deepening into individuality, of promise more than justified in the keeping: unhappy, whose autumn shows only the aftermath and rowen of an earlier harvest, whose would-be replenishments are but thin dilutions of his fame!

The nineteenth century has produced no more purely original writer than Mr. Hawthorne. A shallow criticism has sometimes fancied a resem-

[1] *The Marble Faun.* A Romance of Monte Beni. By NATHANIEL HAWTHORNE. 2 vols. Boston: Ticknor & Fields. 1860.

blance between him and Poe. But it seems to us that the difference between them is the immeasurable one between talent carried to its ultimate, and genius,—between a masterly adaptation of the world of sense and appearance to the purposes of Art, and a so thorough conception of the world of moral realities that Art becomes the interpreter of something profounder than herself. In this respect it is not extravagant to say that Hawthorne has something of kindred with Shakspeare. But that breadth of nature which made Shakspeare incapable of alienation from common human nature and actual life is wanting to Hawthorne. He is rather a denizen than a citizen of what men call the world. We are conscious of a certain remoteness in his writings, as in those of Donne, but with such a difference that we should call the one super- and the other subter-sensual. Hawthorne is psychological and metaphysical. Had he been born without the poetic imagination, he would have written treatises on the Origin of Evil. He does not draw characters, but rather conceives them and then shows them acted upon by crime, passion, or circumstance, as if the element of Fate were as present to his imagination as to that of a Greek dramatist. Helen we know, and Antigone, and Benedick, and Falstaff, and Miranda, and Parson Adams, and Major Pendennis,—these people have walked on pavements or looked out of club-room windows; but what are these idiosyncrasies into which Mr. Hawthorne has breathed a necromantic life, and which he has endowed with the forms and attributes of men? And yet, grant him his premises, that is, let him once get his morbid tendency, whether inherited or the result of special experience, either incarnated as a new man or usurping all the faculties of one already in the flesh, and it is marvelous how subtlely and with what truth to as much of human nature as is included in a diseased consciousness he traces all the finest nerves of impulse and motive, how he compels every trivial circumstance into an accomplice of his art, and makes the sky flame with foreboding or the landscape chill and darken with remorse. It is impossible to think of Hawthorne without at the same time thinking of the few great masters of imaginative composition; his works, only not abstract because he has the genius to make them ideal, belong not specially to our clime or generation; it is their moral purpose alone, and perhaps their sadness, that mark him as the son of New England and the Puritans.

It is commonly true of Hawthorne's romances that the interest centres in one strongly defined protagonist, to whom the other characters are accessory and subordinate,—perhaps we should rather say a ruling Idea, of which all the characters are fragmentary embodiments. They remind us of a symphony of Beethoven's, in which, though there be variety of parts, yet all are infused with the dominant motive, and heighten its impression by hints and far-away suggestions at the most unexpected moment. As in Rome the obelisks are placed at points toward which several streets converge, so in Mr. Hawthorne's stories the actors and incidents seem but vistas through which we see the moral from different points of view,—a moral pointing skyward always, but inscribed with hieroglyphs mysteriously suggestive, whose incitement to conjecture, while they baffle it, we prefer to any prosaic solution.

Nothing could be more original or imaginative than the conception of the character of Donatello in Mr. Hawthorne's new romance. His likeness to the lovely statue of Praxiteles, his happy animal temperament, and the dim legend of his pedigree are combined with wonderful art to reconcile us to the notion of a Greek myth embodied in an Italian of the nineteenth century; and when at length a soul is created in this primeval pagan, this child of earth, this creature of mere instinct, awakened through sin to a conception of the necessity of atonement, we feel, that, while we looked to be entertained with the airiest of fictions, we were dealing with the most august truths of psychology, with the most pregnant facts of modern history, and studying a profound parable of the development of the Christian Idea.

Everything suffers a sea-change in the depths of Mr. Hawthorne's mind, gets rimmed with an impalpable fringe of melancholy moss, and there is a tone of sadness in this book as in the rest, but it does not leave us sad. In a series of remarkable and characteristic works, it is perhaps the most remarkable and characteristic. If you had picked up and read a stray leaf of it anywhere, you would have exclaimed, "Hawthorne!"

The book is steeped in Italian atmosphere. There are many landscapes in it full of breadth and power, and criticisms of pictures and statues always delicate, often profound. In the Preface, Mr. Hawthorne pays a well-deserved tribute of admiration to several of our sculptors, especially to Story and Akers. The hearty enthusiasm with which he elsewhere speaks of the former artist's "Cleopatra" is no surprise to Mr. Story's friends at home, though hardly less gratifying to them than it must be to the sculptor himself.

D'ISRAELI AS A NOVELIST

D'ISRAELI AS A NOVELIST[1]

THE world of the conventional novel is peculiar and apart. It lies somewhere in the same parallels with the land of Cockaigne and the Paradise of Fools. It cannot be far from that district of Spain so thickly dotted with castles erected by non-resident proprietors. The Barbary coast of the piratical cheap-reprinters lies within easy sail of it. Its existence is religiously believed in by thousands who would contemptuously overwhelm one with scientific confutations of the reality of the Lycanthropi and Patagonians. To those whose broad views of life are taken from the speculative heights of the boarding-school attic, or from behind the isolating ramparts of the circulating-library counter, it is far more real than Boston or Cambridge. To them, the manners and customs, the language, costume, and diet, of its inhabitants are more familiar than those of their own neighbors and fellow-citizens. The shameful gibbet of the upturned nose is erected at once for such unworthy persons as are ignorant of its politics and morals. Yet it is a land of comparatively recent discovery. What we know of it is due wholly to modern science and energy. Hakluyt and Purchas are quite vacant in regard to it. We search for it

[1] *Tancred, or the New Crusade, a Novel.* By B. D'ISRAELI, M. P. 1847.

vainly in any *Orbis Depictus.* Peter Martyr tells strange stories, but has described no nation so peculiar. It may possibly have formed part of Mercator's projection, but with him it went no farther than a mere projection, if so far. There is no mention of it in Harris or Pinkerton. Even the voluminous Mavor, the delight of our boyhood, caught sight of it, if ever, only from some Pisgah's top.

The most accurate delineation of it may be found in the works of Bulwer and D'Israeli. Dickens, for a writer of novels, is shamefully uninformed in this particular; Mr. Monks, in Oliver Twist, is the only one of his characters who gives us any direct hint that he is aware of its existence. In general, they impress us as the acting of Garrick did the disappointed and indignant Partridge. We need not look into novels for such; we can meet them every day in the street. It is to the two distinguished authors above named, then, that we are indebted for whatever precise knowledge we have gleaned of this *terra incognita.* Not that they have enriched us with a professedly exact and minute description of it. We must construct our theory of its social peculiarities, as we re-create the private life of the Greeks, from the incidental *data* let fall by those in whose eyes objects had lost their sharp outline by familiarity. So much of preface seemed necessary to excuse the too evident incompleteness of our sketch.

The first peculiar characteristic of the inhabitants of this shadowy region is their longevity.

They realize what was, at best, only theoretic with Pythagoras. This antediluvian prolixity is accompanied, and perhaps deprived of its monotony, by a Cerberus-like capacity of being several gentlemen at once. Thus, the identical False Messiah of the "Wondrous Tale of Alroy" turns up again, after several centuries of withdrawal into private life, in the person of Vivian Grey. Again we encounter him, with scarcely even an attempt at *incognito,* performing contemporaneously the functions (fortunately not very onerous) of Coningsby, Sidonia, Tancred, and we know not how many others. We are quite confident that we detect him as Mr. Leander, the culinary artist of the New Crusade. In the same manner, Eugene Aram, of whom the last penalty of the law would seem to have rid us in a constitutional and thorough manner, reappears again as Zanoni, and we afterwards find that he had in the meanwhile imposed himself on a too facile public as something new, under the several *aliases* of Paul Clifford, Pelham, and Maltravers. To be sure, as Zanoni, he offers a lame kind of apology for his conduct, by professing to have discovered the *aurum potabile;* but he can hardly expect to escape much longer the vigilance of the literary police.

The distinguished authors from whom our examples have been taken seem to have forgotten, in their familiarity with this patriarchal tenacity of life, the impoverished and more limited date of their readers. They have unconsciously adapted themselves, in the profusion of their works and the rapidity with which one follows another, to a style of living which finds its nearest modern parallel in the famous Countess of Desmond,

> "Who lived to the age of a hundred and ten,
> And died by a fall from an apple-tree then."

The writing of books of this kind is comparatively an easy matter, but the reading demands a more liberal outlay of energy and persistency. Had the crowning labor of Hercules been to keep pace with the pen of an author like Mr. G. P. R. James, he would probably not even yet have seen his name gazetted for a place on Olympus. It is possible, that, among the improvements of science, a machine may be invented for the more rapid perusal of this kind of literature. Delusive hopes have sometimes been awakened in us by seeing advertisements of "Reading made easy." Babbage's calculating-machine supplies very creditably, in scientific circles, the places of some score of mathematicians, but the remedy for our especial complaint is not to be found in the pharmacopœia of mechanics. The great want of an age always foretells, and in some sort defines, its great invention; and we may therefore look pretty confidently for the speedy introduction of a labor-saving engine, which shall meet the demands of an overworked public. Formerly, authors were more considerate. It is plain that Richardson calculated his Sir Charles Grandison for the longest period of years attainable in his day. No other reason is assignable for the story's ending where it does, or indeed at all. To a lover of statistics there is something touching in a concession like this to the tables of longevity. The matter assumes something of a grand and Roman aspect, when we picture to ourselves the stoical conscientiousness with which he brought his work to an end, lest any reader, who might fall a little short of the required period, should miss the conclusion, and die feeling defrauded of his proper pennyworth.

We cannot be expected to give anything more than a meagre sketch of the interesting race of beings of whom we were treating at the other end of our digression, and to whose consideration we now return. It may be well to premise, that, besides the particular names with which they are labeled for the sake of convenient distinction (a precaution rendered necessary by their singular family-likeness one to another), they are also known by one universal patronymic. Each male is called a Hero, and each female a Heroine. It may be, that, in common with all races who have achieved eminence, they ascribe to themselves a mythical inception. Generally, the fable typified the character of the people. The she-wolf's milk would not out of the Roman blood, and the Athenian could trace the transmitted qualities of his ancestral grasshopper in his own fickle and mercurial temperament. The tribe under consideration may claim an origin in the famous intimacy of Hero and Leander, assuming the name of its maternal ancestor, according to the principles of the common law, for want of a marriage certificate. The early demise of Hero furnishes no valid argument against this theory. Every day we see genealogists of enthusiasm and fortitude cheerfully surmounting far more serious obstacles. At least, if this be not the true solution of the problem, a just deference to the principles of language will allow us to seek it nowhere else. No recognized definition of the word "Hero" will meet the wants of the case.

It has been assumed too rashly by ethical writers, that no race of men can be found among whom there does not exist some idea, however rude, of a deity, a future state of existence, and a moral law. Wilson detected traces of a sense of justice even among martins; and we remember reading in some books of travels an account of a funeral procession of apes, concluding with an *éloge* pronounced at the grave by a distinguished member of the Simial Academy,—which learned body, like other foreign scientific and literary societies, has doubtless its corresponding members in the United States, though we have hitherto failed to detect its *insignia* in the mystical abbreviations of title-page literature, or in the Ciceronian Latin of college catalogues. However this may be, we have been unable to find any distinct recognition of a God or a code of morals among the peculiar people whose habits we are investigating. The only symptom of respect even for the prejudices of society which they exhibit is to be found in their almost invariably claiming a descent from some ancient and generally noble family. It is not impossible that the goddess Vacuna may be worshipped among them. They are generally said to be learned and philosophical; but the possession of these qualities hardly comports with their habits of life, and the story wants ampler confirmation than we have yet seen. It certainly is not at all sustained by any of their reported speeches or deeds.

If what we have surmised of their longevity be true, it will elucidate another circumstance otherwise mysterious. We allude to the indefiniteness of their ideas concerning time. Those little items in the expenditure of this precious commodity, over which a man would hesitate whose income was determinable by the seignioral whim of death, are quite lightly esteemed by those whose lives are not dependent on the ordinary contingencies of mortality. Thus, in their books, we constantly meet with statements like this:—"On a fine afternoon in the year 16—, a youth whose etc., etc. *might* bespeak him to be of the age of twenty-five or thereabout;"—or, "On a breezy September afternoon in the year 18—, a man whose immaculate boots suitably terminated a costume of singular etc., etc. *might have been* seen." In this way we are provokingly arrested on the very threshold of precise knowledge, and the conditional expression leaves us in a painful state of suspense. Everything becomes at once vague and phantasmal, like the banquet of a Lamia, and the illusory viands which had satisfied our intellectual appetites, as long as we partook of them in good faith, gripe us with a retrospective starvation.

Several physiological peculiarities are sufficiently well established in regard to the subjects of our somewhat erratic investigation. We know theoretically that all mankind naturally behold objects reversed, and only correct this apparently needless optical ceremony by an unconscious act of reason. This process of reasoning is rejected by these people as superfluous and artificial; and there is something not unrefreshing to a mind accustomed to our conventional distinctions in noting the impressions and studying the mental habits of those to whom all objects, especially in morals, present themselves invariably upside down. While upon the subject of optics, we may remark, also, that their looks always contain a volume of meaning (certainly not one of the volumes of either of the famous authors from whom we chiefly draw our information), a compensation doubtless intended by even-handed Nature to make up for the preternatural vacuity of their speech. One other fact is singular enough to be commented on here. All their male children are born with silver spoons in their mouths. This accounts for their always marrying heiresses, or succeeding to immense estates early in life, and throws all the responsibility for a seemingly unequal distribution of material blessings upon the ample shoulders of natural causes. It has been supposed by many, that these curious appendages of nativity are ladles, or at least spoons of more Homeric dimensions than any we are familiar with. This may, however, be merely a theoretic adaptation of antecedent to consequence, arising from an effort of logical minds to graduate the size of the spoon to the amount of luck contingent upon it. It should never be forgotten, that this sublime species is not amenable to any of those influences which are dominant in our more limited organizations. Certain it is, that none of them possess the happy faculty of being poor. No translation would make intelligible to them the

"vitæ tuta facultas
Pauperis."

We have not been able to discover that they devote themselves to any of the professions which are considered reputable among us. The life of a brigand is clearly not liable to reproach among them, and they not infrequently present examples of dandies with immeasurable aspirations, æsthetic assassins, and thieves from a devotion to the sublime and beautiful. Within a few years they have begun to adapt themselves to the general tendency toward Reform; and here they have exhibited an almost celestial unselfishness, appropriating all their efforts to the defects of their neighbors, and leaving their own to divine interposition and providential ravens. Their women differ not greatly from the other sex. Perhaps the profound author of "Woman in the Nineteenth Century" designed to typify them under the class of women of "electric organizations," concerning whom she utters many mysterious oracles. Perhaps the laws of this phenomenal society forbade her being more definite. In Silliman's Journal there was published, several years ago, an account of a lady in Vermont who emitted sparks whenever she approached any metallic substance. A closer analysis of this case might possibly throw some light on the matter.

It may be, that there is no particular locality inhabited by this interesting tribe, where they constitute a distinct people, governed by their own laws, and free to carry out their own principles of action. It has sometimes occurred to us, that they might possibly exist among ourselves, like the Jews in Spain, or like the brethren of the mysterious Vehm and of the Rose Cross in Germany, subjecting our more commonplace existence to the criterion of their sublimer ideal. They resemble the Rosicrucians in using a kind of cryptography totally destitute of meaning to the unilluminated eye, but differ from them again in regard to the sacred numbers, holding only Number One in peculiar veneration. We have fancied sometimes, that we could detect, in the countenances of young gentlemen who measured us a yard of tape, what would be called by their cabalistic writers a mysterious something, indicating a sense of awful responsibility, and a half-melancholy, half-contemptuous superiority to the drudgery whose convenient disguise they have assumed. It is not unlikely, that members of the guild may be found among that lazzaroni class of our population who fish from the bridges and wharves, or more probably in those who watch and criticize the piscatory endeavors of others. This surmise finds confirmation in their entire want of any useful employment whatever, in their use of a dialect semi-unintelligible to the ordinary hearer, and their sublime indifference to those limited theories of government and reform which obtain in the community of which they consent to appear members. Their hands are commonly thrust deep into their pockets, as if in contemptuous defiance of the primal curse, or in tacit assumption of some higher than an Adamite original. Their costume, also, is at once negligent and graceful, and less indicative of a slavish dependence upon the tailor, than of the inventive embroideries of private taste and original views in art.—But we must leave this tempting theme, and let ourselves down gradually to the subject of our present article.

The palmy days of the novel are gone forever. Its age is passed, like that of chivalry, whose decadence Burke could lament, but whose precise place in history he would have been puzzled to define. The world is not what it was when Byron wrote to England for the last Scotch novel, and lazy Coleridge felt grumblingly constrained to read it by a kind of Ancient Mariner's spell. The invention of printing, which brought down the apple of knowledge within the reach of all, seems to have entailed likewise upon mankind a laborious curse akin to that which ensued from the original bite, and it is only within a few years that men have begun to ask themselves why they read. The patience of mankind in this particular makes Job no longer exceptional. "Chappelow on Job" is a sorer trial than ever visited the patriarch himself. A modern degeneracy wonders at the heroic age which took "Calvinus *in Prophetas*" and "Vitringa *in Esaiam*" as matters of course. That men should have conquered Dwight's Conquest of Canaan seems now as prodigious a thing as the great achievement of Cortez himself; and the journal of some worthy Bernal Diaz who took part in the enterprise would be an interesting record of devotion and courage. We ourselves once, infected with Wertherism, began to peruse Morse on Suicide, as a convenient, and not inadequate, substitute for the thing itself. We are apt to look upon such books as the megatheria of literature; but the race of dodos survives to connect us with an otherwise extinct epoch. Have we not our commentators upon Shakspeare? Have we not our almost hourly novels? Have we not our periodic inflictions, from the daily newspaper up to the quarterly, the multicaulis of the species? Nevertheless, the reign of the novelists was over, like that of the Barbary corsairs, as soon as Christendom began to inquire whether there was any foreordained necessity for submitting to their exactions. Literature has taken what is called a useful direction, and the romantic fiction of the traveler is gradually crowding out that of the novelist.

In point of fact, also, the gradual exclusion of the novelist from the improbable, and his confinement to the region of every-day life, amount to a kind of prohibitory statute against all but men of genuine creative power. We can show nothing now that will compare in kind with the romantic dreams of our ancestors. The exploration and settlement of this Western world, while they have added myriads to the circle of the story-teller, have at the same time robbed romance of one of its widest and most enticing fields. The age of expectation is past. It is true that English travelers among us have endeavored to ignore the silent flight of centuries and the uncompromising advance of exact knowledge, and have continued to write in the imaginative strain of those voyagers who adventured at a period when geography and general science were in a state of more fortunate obscurity. But the mariner no longer hoists confident sail for El Dorado. No Ponce de Leon ravishes the virgin silence of embowered rivers in believing search for the fountain of youth, a fountain in whose existence the ever-young fancy of that unskeptical age might almost tempt us to put faith. No English crew, trailing with sleepy canvas through those sun-steeped seas,

> "Where the remote Bermudas ride
> In the ocean's bosom unespied,"

can dream of the Marquis of the Valley, and of empires overrun by a handful of Buccaneers, with any substantial hope of emulating that Aladdin-like fortunateness, nor can they bring home tales out of which such "golden exhalations of the dawn" as Ariel can be created. Stephens, to be sure, with a praiseworthy endeavor after such precious credulity, tells stories of undiscovered cities in Central America, incapable of entrapping our boys of the lowest form. The discovery of a new plant, bird, or insect is the sole reward of modern adventure. We must perforce be content that an addition to our authentic Flora or Fauna shall repay us for the loss we suffer in the diminished empire of the unknown and mysterious. The mere potential possession of those wondrous efficacies which were once believed to dwell in plants and minerals, of those untraversed empires ribbed with gold which waited for conquerors, was in itself a great estate to be born to, the loss of which finds but a beggarly compensation in any accession of preciser science. The index to Browne's Vulgar Errors is a meagre inventory of those vast possessions out of which the advance of knowledge has juggled us. Even among the stars, speculation is no longer safe. The astronomer, drifting on his telescope through the sea of space, finds every gleaming continent, every nebulous Polynesian group, already taken possession of in the name of some European power.

The present age, we are constantly assured, is an age of criticism and inquiry, quite barren of the beautiful, childlike faith of the bygone time. We are well content that it should be so, while we can see a higher and more saving grace gradually unfolding itself. We shall not feel that there is any loss, so long as a faith in the present and the future, in man and his true destiny, takes the place of the old religion. Out of the decay of no system can we reproduce its original type. There is nourishment only for a fungous and inferior life. One epoch is but the sheath which envelopes and protects the flower-bud of the next; the expanding blossom detrudes it. Experience may be the best schoolmaster, but where is the instance in history of a generation in whom his birch implanted any wisdom? At best, his qualities are negative, and he teaches rather what to avoid than what to do. Yet there is in England a political party, or a spasmodic attempt at one, based upon the dogma that all salvation dwells in the past. Mr. D'Israeli the younger is one of the Coryphæi of this sect, and Tancred is one of its canonical books. It calls itself "Young England," and we should be inclined to consider it very young indeed, if we might judge by the clearest apprehension we have been able to attain of the principles by which it professes to be governed. It claims to be the friend of reform, but seems to look upon progress as something of the same nature with the refractory charge of an Irish pig-driver, and pulls it back stoutly by the leg in a direction precisely the reverse of that in which it would have it advance. Coningsby, Sibyl, and Tancred are samples of its literature. Of its Parliamentary oratory the staple seems to be a series of assaults upon Sir Robert Peel for the wisest act of his life, in yielding to the progress of events. These onslaughts are of the style usually called "withering"; but from his remarks on the Irish question, we should suppose the late Premier to be as verdant as ever.

The "Young England" party is apparently made up of something like a dozen middle-aged gentlemen, either members of Parliament, or conceiving themselves eminently adapted for a seat in that assembly. They are persuaded that there has been, at some time or other (they are somewhat vague on this point), a golden age in England. They are satisfied that John Bull must be made a boy again, that all work and no play have made Jack a dull boy. But in what Medea's caldron they would boil the allegorical old gentleman we are not informed. That the result of the experiment would not be more fortunate than that of the daughters of Pelias, we can readily believe. They do not define exactly the happy oasis in the desert of history to which they would return. Perhaps it may be located not far from the time of the publication of the Book of Sports. They would restore the happy days of the peasantry, by setting them to climb greased poles, or race in sacks. An occasional game of skittles would at once elevate the condition and fill the bellies of the operatives. Squires Butler, Smith, and Cook, otherwise rather unendurable country-gentlemen, would be transformed into liberal and enlightened citizens, as Messrs. Boteler, Smythe, and Coke. Hollow-cheeked want and abysmal ignorance, in a frieze jacket and corduroy smalls, would become plump satiety and Arcadian simplicity, in a doublet and hose. They seem all to have been born under the dominance of Cancer, and, walking steadfastly backward, would persuade us, like Cacus, to take the direction of their footprints as ample evidence of an advance the other way. They have an appearance of wisdom sufficient to captivate the greener sort of boys. The enunciation of the simplest fact wears with them the air of a discovery, and the words must begin with capitals to be adequate to the occasion. They suppose an ignorance in their readers which would perhaps have overtaxed that humility of the old philosopher who considered his education complete when he had learned at last that he knew nothing. They talk of absolute principles as familiarly as a snob quotes his distinguished acquaintances, his nearest intimacy with whom, perhaps, has been the writing to them for an autograph and getting no reply. They criticize the present condition of affairs, and, when asked for a remedy, their answer is as satisfactory as that with which contemptuous boys refer the snowballed passer-by, who proves refractory, to the town-pump for sympathy and redress. They find the pulse of the body politic alarming, and prescribe ten drops of the tincture of the Middle Ages. Alas for poor Sancho, if once seduced into a trial of this Quixotic balsam! Is Ireland starving? They would order iron, by way of tonic, and prevent any recurrence of unfavorable symptoms by a strong infusion of railroads, beginning nowhere, running nowhere else, and carrying nothing but a conviction of the imbecility of government. Like a barometer from an auction-sale, they inflexibly indicate a storm brewing, nor can any length of sunshine avail to mollify their contumacious vaticination of foul weather. They have a prodigious command of phrases. They affirm this and that, and deny the other, of any given subject, and, after wholly bemuddling the too trustful reader, who, with open mouth and shut eyes, sincerely expects something to make him wise, complete their victory and his mortification by naming the process a rigorous analysis,—emulating the hardihood of that equestrian nominalist who

> "Stuck a feather in his hat
> And *called* it macaroni."

They overwhelm us with "objective" and "subjective," with "combinations," "problems," and "developments," till we are fain to believe in our own ignorance rather than credit the boldness and profundity of theirs. They are of the school of Diphilus the Labyrinth, whom we met once in Lucian's Lapithæ. Their truths are invariably stranger than any but their own fictions. Their method of argument reminds one of Lord Humevesne's plea:—"If the iniquity of men were as easily seen in categorical judgment as we can discern flies in a milk-pot, the world's four oxen had not been so eaten up with rats, nor had so many ears been nibbled away so scurvily." They, however, do not appear to have undergone any such auricular curtailment. They profess an entire confidence in the efficacy of Faith, and charge all the world's troubles to a backsliding in that particular. This Faith they seem to regard as something capable of manufacture, and not beyond the cunning of Manchester or Sheffield. Their best type in America is Mr. Brownson (*male tutæ mentis Orestes*), who, nailing at length his weary weathercock to the mast, and gulping down with an equable countenance œcumenical councils, cardinals, popes, whole hecatombs of papal bulls, and (more than all) his own previous writings, would persuade the public, by an exhibition of his own marvelous feats in that kind, to the more hazardous experiment of swallowing himself and his pretensions.

But Mr. D'Israeli is not a gentleman of sufficiently assured position to wait patiently in the antechamber, and it is time that we should apply ourselves personally to him. He is a great believer in the idiosyncrasies of race, and the peculiar tendencies and faculties implanted in the different families of mankind. He himself furnishes an unconscious illustration of his own theory. Seldom has the inner life been so aptly symbolized in the outward as in the case of the Jews. That the idolaters of ceremony and tradition should become the venders of old clothes, that the descendants of those who, within earshot of the thunders of Sinai, could kneel before the golden calf, should be the money-changers of Europe, has in it something of syllogistic completeness. The work by which the elder D'Israeli will be remembered is the old curiosity shop of literature. He is merely a cast-clothesdealer in an æsthetic sense. The son, with his trumpery of the past, is clearly a vender of the same wares, and an offshoot from the same stock.

In Coningsby and Tancred, Mr. D'Israeli has interwoven a kind of defense of the Jewish race against the absurd prejudices of a so-called Christendom. The Arab proves his unmixed descent by the arch of his instep; and, unless we conclude men mad as sturdy old Burton argues them, we must suppose that the pleasurable sensation of pedigree has somewhere its peculiar organ in the human frame. With proper deference to the opinions of other physiologists, we should be inclined to place the seat of this emotion in the Caucasian race near the region of the toes. Tribes of this stock, at least, have always seemed to consider the keeping of somebody or other to kick as at once a proof of purity of lineage, and a suitable gratification of those nobler instincts which it implants. In Europe, the Jews have long monopolized the responsible privilege of supplying an object for this peculiar craving of the supreme Caucasian nature. The necessity of each rank in society found a vent upon that next below it, the diapason ending full in the Jew; and thus a healthy feeling of dignity was maintained from one end of the body politic to the other. In America, the African supplies the place of the Hebrew, and the sturdiest champion of impartial liberty feels the chromatic scale of equal rights violated when the same steam is employed to drag him and his darker fellow-citizen. Civilization has made wonderful advances since the apostle Philip mounted the chariot of the Ethiopian eunuch. It must be remembered, however, that Ethiopians do not keep chariots nowadays.

For once, Mr. D'Israeli seems to be in earnest, and we respect both his zeal and the occasion of it. The pen is never so sacred as when it takes the place of the sword in securing freedom, whether for races or ideas. But the earnestness of a charlatan is only a profounder kind of charlatanism. The moral of Tancred, if it have any, is, that effete Europe can be renewed only by a fresh infusion from the veins of Asia,—a nostrum for rejuvenescence to be matched only out of the pages of Hermippus Redivivus. According to Mr. D'Israeli, all primitive ideas have originated, and must forever originate, in Asia, and among the descendants of Abraham. He would have us go to school to Noah in navigation, and learn the nicer distinctions of *meum* and *tuum* from Ishmael. He would make us believe that the Jewish mind still governs the world, through the medium of prime-ministers, bankers, and actresses. The chief excellence of this arrangement is, that we are profoundly ignorant of it. We are provided for by the supreme Arabian intellect, and at the same time have all the pleasure of imagining that we manage our own affairs. The dispersion of the Jews (a nation so eminently successful in controlling their own political interests) was no doubt intended by Providence to supply Christendom with administrative intellects.

In simple truth, it seems to have been a provision of nature that divine ideas should have been committed to the Jews, as great fortunes come to unthrift heirs, because they were unable to keep possession of them. The world is indeed too much governed by the Jewish mind, though not in the sense Mr. D'Israeli intended. Instead of the absolute truth, it accepts the corrupt Hebrew gloss. The Jews were never able to look an organic truth full in the face. They could not even behold clearly the countenance of their first great lawgiver, for the brightness that encompassed it; much less could they discern the more purely effulgent lineaments of Jesus. The Gospels are still too often read backward, after the Hebrew fashion.

Mr. D'Israeli would be more endurable, if he himself thoroughly believed in the theory he promulgates. But it is evident that he only assumes his position for the sake of writing what one half of May Fair shall pronounce brilliant, and the other half profound. An original kind of originality has lately been discovered, which consists in asserting sheer nonsense, and then compassionating the incredulous reader's want of brains. The old scientific writers used to define white as *disgregativum visûs,* something which dissipated and puzzled the sight. A kind of writing has obtained of late which realizes this definition. It is called the brilliant style, and has at least this property of brilliancy, that the eye strives in vain to settle upon and clutch any definite object. The natural philosopher would be posed to find a substance in which the mass bore so small a proportion to the volume, or, to speak more properly, the number of volumes. It is painful reading. The wearied attention can alight nowhere. Getting through books constructed on this principle is like crossing a stream upon blocks of ice, each one of which admits of being skimmed lightly over, but where a pause insures hopeless submersion. Arrived on the other side, we have no distinct consciousness except of being over, and can only congratulate ourselves upon our happy preservation. It is a feat which demands as much presence of mind in the reader as it implies an absence of that quality in the writer. When such productions are called works of fiction, we cannot complain of being cheated. They have been subjected to no natural period of gestation, and acknowledge no received laws of birth. They are constructed after the manner of Paracelsus's *homunculus,* and are as near of kin to true works of art as the trees in apothecaries' jars are to the pines on Katahdin. There is enough artifice, but no art. Dryden, in a letter to Dennis, says,—"I remember poor Nat Lee, who was upon the verge of madness, yet made a sober and witty answer to a bad poet who told him, 'It was an easy thing to write like a madman.' 'No,' said he, ' 'tis very difficult to write like a madman, but 'tis a very easy thing to write like a fool.' "

We should not be so severe in our exactions of the novel, except that it no longer professes to amuse, but to instruct. This is the age of lectures. Even Punch has got into the professor's chair, and donned the doctor's cap. The novel has become a quack advertisement in three volumes. Formerly, we could detect the political economist at a reasonable distance, and escape him by a well-contrived dodge. Now, no sanctuary is inviolate. Adam Smith gets us inexorably by the button in the corner of some shilling novel, and Malthus entraps us from behind the unsuspected ambush of the last new poem. Even the tragic Muse drops her mask, and behold, Mr. Ricardo! It is getting past endurance. Chandler's History of Persecution supplies no instance more atrocious. The novelist has turned *colporteur* to some board of political missions, and the propagandist of every philosophical soup-and-bread society assumes the disguise of a poet. The times are well-nigh as bad as those a century and a half ago, when our forefathers were fain to carry their firelocks to meeting. Everywhere are surprisals. One cannot saunter down what were once the green lanes or deep withdrawn woodpaths of literature, without being set upon by a whooping band of savages, who knock one on the head with the balance of trade, or tomahawk one with merciless statistics. Everywhere pure literature seems defunct. Art for the sole sake of art is no more. Beauty is no longer "its own excuse for being." It must have a certificate of membership from the Anti-something or Anti-everything Alliance.

Let us not be misapprehended. Divine is the marriage of beauty and use; them God hath joined. The crowning and consummate grace of the Muse is the pouring of wine and oil. She has walked before every higher aspiration, every more generous hope of humanity. Fetters which the dumb tears of ages have not availed to rust in twain have fallen asunder at her look. What she has done has been from a beautiful necessity of her nature. But a Muse with an enforced sense of duty! A Muse in a Quaker bonnet! A Muse who quotes McCulloch! *Quousque tandem?* And the only consolation vouchsafed us is that ours is an age of transition. Let those draw comfort from the thought of belonging to the miocene period who are capable of such cosmogonic satisfactions. To us, it is no relief that we shall have our shelf hereafter in the geologist's cabinet; we cover no fossil immortality.

Mr. D'Israeli began his literary career as an amusing writer merely. He was no unmeet Homer for a dandy Achilles, whose sublime was impertinence. His Vivian Grey, no doubt, made some score of sophomores intolerable in the domestic circle; his Young Duke tempted as many freshmen to overrun their incomes. Nature is said to love a balance of qualities or properties, and to make up always for a deficiency in one place by an excess in some other. But our experience of mankind would incline us to doubt the possible existence of so large a number of modest men as would account for the intensity of Mr. D'Israeli's vicarious atonement. It is painful to conceive of an amount of bashfulness demanding such a counterpoise of assurance. It would seem that he must have borrowed brass, that he must be supporting his lavish expenditures *aere alieno,* when he assumes the philosopher, and undertakes to instruct.

His "New Crusade" can be undertaken by no one short of a duke's only son. It would doubtless be considered a highly revolutionary interference with the vested rights of the aristocracy to allow so great a privilege to a commoner. Tancred is a young gentleman of extraordinary genius and acquirements, just coming of age when the novel opens. His father, the Duke of Bellamont, wishes him to enter Parliament, but he has already resolved on undertaking a pilgrimage to the Holy Sepulchre. Fathers are among the inconvenient necessities of our fallen nature, but an unmanly yielding to them is not one of the weaknesses of the "New Generation." It is probable that they would not be put up with at all, were it not for certain facilities they afford as bankers. Young England respects the fathers of the church vastly more than its own. Tancred, of course, has his own way, and the Duke surrenders at discretion.

The old painters wrote under their honest, but often unsatisfactory, attempts at imitating nature the names of the objects they intended to represent. The moderns have a convenient fetch to accomplish the same end, by means of descriptive catalogues, so that we can assure ourselves at once, that this indescribable phenomenon is the "portrait of a gentleman," and that inscrutably dark canvas, with a dab of white putty in the centre, "is *after* Rembrandt," and can form our own conclusions as to whether it is likely to overtake him. This expedient, as it were, shifts the burden of proof, and taxes rather the imagination and faith of the beholder than the skill of the artist. Yet even here a kind of remote verisimilitude is demanded. Mr. D'Israeli forgets this. He assures us that he is about to introduce a most extraordinary man, a kind of admirabler Crichton. We prepare our minds adequately for the encounter, and then—enter Mr. Sidonia. We are reminded of a placard we once saw, announcing the rather anomalous exhibition of "Colonel Spofford, the *great* Virginia dwarf." We are outraged at so Barmecide a fulfilment of a bill of fare which would have made even Mrs. Glasse search her coffers round. We had always conceived of Nature as somewhat economical and housewifely in her management, expending nothing but for some adequate return. What object she could have had in endowing Mr. Sidonia with so many rare and exceptional qualities, we are at a loss to discover. He talks and acts very much like any other quite ordinary person. His vast faculties seem as superfluous as the five horses which the circus-rider contrives to use at the same time, when one would serve his turn as well. Shakspeare wrote on quite another system. He lets us know, indeed, that Hamlet is "fat and scant o' breath," but leaves Hamlet's genius to speak for itself. Mr. D'Israeli is like the Irish gastronomer, who invited his friends to partake of a rich soup which he was to concoct out of a miraculous pebble. The entertainer liberally placed his whole mineralogical cabinet at the service of his guests, merely asking of each in return a *pro ratâ* contribution of a bit of beef, a trifle of pork, a few onions, a sprinkling of salt, and a kettle wherein to try the thaumaturgic experiment. Mr. D'Israeli's characters are such wonderful pebbles. It is quite too heavy a tax upon the reader to expect him to fill up, with their appropriate lights and shades, the colossal outlines sketched by the author.

Tancred is one of these remarkable men, but there is nothing very remarkable in what he says or does. In the same way that old Gower enters as Chorus, and gives us to understand that we are now in Tyre, Mr. D'Israeli begs to inform us that we are now to enjoy the privilege of communion with a mind capable of vast "combinations." But Tyre turns out to be the same little canvas castle which was Tharsus a moment ago, and the vast combinations amount to the adding of two and two, and producing the surprising result of four. We had calculated upon ten, at the very least. Tancred goes to the Holy Land to fathom the great "Asiatic problem," carrying, one cannot help fearing, a line hardly long enough for the purpose. Arrived there, he pays his devotion to the Holy Sepulchre, undertakes a pilgrimage to

Mount Sinai, is taken prisoner by a tribe of Arabs descended from Rechab (the temperance reform may be allegorically typified in this incident), is liberated, visits the Ansarey, a somewhat anserine people who maintain the worship of the Grecian divinities, and the novel ends by his declaring his love for the daughter of his Jew banker in Palestine. The conclusion is characteristic. Mr. D'Israeli, like the cat transformed into a lady, drops all ceremony at once, and makes a joyous spring after the first mouse he encounters. The novelist gets the better of the philosopher.

If the book were intended as a satire, the end would be pertinent enough. But in the present case, it is as if a man, with infinite din of preparation, should set sail for a voyage round the world, and get no farther than a chowder on Spectacle Island. At the beginning of the novel, we nerve ourselves for the solution of the great Asiatic problem, and, as long as *X* remains an unknown quantity, we feel a vague sort of respect for it. But when we arrive at the end of the demonstration, and Mr. D'Israeli, after covering the blackboard with figures enough to work out the position of the new planet, turns round to us, and, laying down his triumphant chalk, says gravely,—"Thus, Gentlemen, you will perceive that the square of the hypotenuse, &c., &c., Q. E. D.," we feel as if we might have found our way over the *pons asinorum* without paying him so heavy a fee as guide. He finds a prototype in Lilly the astrologer, who, commending his own calling, asserts roundly, that "the study required in that kind of learning must be sedentary, of great reading, sound judgment, which no man can accomplish except he wholly retire, use prayer, and accompany himself with angelical visitations." This impresses us considerably, till we reflect that all this machinery is put in motion, not to produce a *Novum Organon,* but to track a stolen spoon, or to estimate the chances of recovering an absconded sixpence.

The value of any book, after all, is not in the entertainment it affords for the nonce, though this is something, but in the permanent residuum left in the mind after reading. The times are too much in earnest for abandonment to simple recreation. Were this not so, the imitations of Punch, *at* which, would answer the same purpose as Punch itself, *with* which we laugh. The solid residuum we speak of depends upon the amount of thinking which the book has demanded of us. That which the old epitaph affirms of worldly goods holds true here also,—what we gave we have. The intellect seeks food, and would reject all the pearls in the world for a single grain of corn. Art is only conscious Nature, and Nature has always her ulterior views, creating nothing but with an eye to some desired result. But Tancred cannot be esteemed a work of art, even if that term may be justly applied in the limited sense of mere construction. There is in it no great living idea which pervades, molds, and severely limits the whole. If we consider the *motive,* we find a young nobleman so disgusted with the artificial and hollow life around him, that he sacrifices everything for a pilgrimage to what he believes the only legitimate source of faith and inspiration. We cannot, to be sure, expect much of a youth who is obliged to travel a thousand miles after inspiration; but we might reasonably demand something more than that he should merely fall in love, a consummation not less conveniently and cheaply attainable at home. If the whole story be intended for a satire, the disproportion of motive to result is not out of proper keeping. But Mr. D'Israeli's satire is wholly of the epigrammatic kind, not of the epic, and deals always with individuals, never with representative ideas. An epigram in three volumes post octavo is out of the question. The catastrophe has no moral or æsthetic fitness. Indeed, there is no principle of cohesion about the book, if we except the covers. Nor could there be; for there is no one central thought around and toward which the rest may gravitate. All that binds the incidents together is the author's will, a somewhat inadequate substitute for a law of nature. Everything slips through our fingers like a handful of sand, when we grasp for a design. A true work of art is like a tree. Its shape, its law of growth, its limit, is irrevocably foreordained in the seed. There is no haphazard in the matter, from beginning to end. The germ once planted, everything then tends simply to the bringing about of one end,—perfection in its kind. The plot which it has to fill out is definite and rigid. The characters and incidents balance each other like the branches, and every part, from the minutest fibre of the root to the least leaf, conspires to nourishment and so to beauty. The grand, yet simple pose, the self-possession, so to speak, is what impresses us with a sense of dignity and permanence. We come to criticize it, and feel as if brought before it to be criticized rather. It turns the tables upon us and demands our credentials. But to call upon Mr. D'Israeli for a work of art is to set a joiner to build an oak.

For want of due discrimination, such writers as Mr. D'Israeli are called *imaginative* authors. It is the same narrow view which has confined the name of poets to the makers of verse. Imagination is truly the highest exercise of that august faculty from which it is vulgarly esteemed so distant,—namely, reason. It is the instinctive (if we may so call it, in the absence of any readier term) perception of remote analogies; in other words, of the unity of truth. It has been said of Shakspeare, the greatest imagination in the history of literature, that as much reasoning faculty was required for the production of one of his dramas as for that of the *Novum Organon.* According to our view of the matter, Bacon's great work indicates the presence of an imagination only second to that which found its natural outlet in Hamlet and Lear. Many examples, were it necessary, might be brought to prove that the great mathematical or scientific mind is not so different in kind from the poetical as is generally taken for granted. It will be enough if we merely mention Pascal and Davy. The theory had its rise among a race of third-rate rhymers, who found it convenient to persuade the world that the payment of debts and the possession of genius were two luxuries whose simultaneous enjoyment was impossible. A generation which tolerated such poets might easily be put off with such crambo stuff for philosophy. Swedenborg, whose imaginative powers will hardly be questioned, is just beginning to be understood as the profoundest scientific writer of his age. Any one who reads him will perceive that he is wholly wanting in fancy. Voltaire, a writer of pure fancy, with no trace of imagination, and whose mind therefore detected incongruities well enough, but could never rise to the perception of harmonic laws, naturally applied to Shakspeare the ludicrous epithet of *bizarre*. The same term would have served him equally well for the solar system. Imagination made the one, when he chose, a great satirist. Fancy, which places side by side in piquant comparison remotely allied images, not ideas, made the other, whether he would or no, a great epigrammatist.

Imagination has been truly and wisely named "the shaping spirit." It is this that gives unity to the otherwise formless mass, and inspires it with one decisive and harmonious will. Without it there may be great power, but no unity,—only agglomeration. Herein lies the distinction between Shakspeare and Marlowe. The latter is commonly labeled by the critics as a poet of wild and lawless imagination, a definition which seems to us as idle as if one should say a wild and lawless definition. For nothing is great or beautiful which is lawless, and we must be careful that we do not name that so which is truly subjected to some law so high or so refined as to transcend or elude the ordinary apprehension. The imagination acts within certain prescribed and absolute limits, and we believe that in all literature no instance of its pure exercise can be adduced, which is not at the same time an example of the highest reason. We do not mean to assert a paradox when we say that the versification of Shakspeare often displays imagination, while the sentiment embodied in it is purely fanciful; since it is this faculty which gives form, and subjects expression to those higher principles of order and unity of which fancy is altogether incapable. It is from a want of fixed ideas as to the operations of this attribute of the profoundest intellect, that the fallacy of great wit being nearly allied to madness has arisen. For the imagination necessarily oversteps the narrow limits which circumscribe the general mind, and therefore seems something abnormal and erratic. A more exact astronomy teaches that the long ellipse of the comet is governed by principles as exact, and characterized by periods as uniform, as the seemingly more regular planetary orbits. The mental organization of great reformers has imagination for its basis, but in them it is rather a quality than a faculty, and they are convicted of being men of one idea by a populace which is often not fortunate enough to possess even one, because they are constantly testing what is by what ought to be, and subjecting the fugitive forms of society, in which Truth disguises herself for a time, to the touchstone of absolute reason.

There is a kind of criticism which judges books by their own aim, and which answers very well where the having any definite intent may be predicated of the book in hand. But this has been perverted from its true scope to cover the defects of every false and empty school of literature that has ever arisen. It is then called liberal criticism, a term which, like liberal Christianity, often means either a very illiberal criticism or none at all. Thus plentifully infused with water, the test is applied, and accommodatingly indicates the presence of whatever quality is desired. It is like the gimlet of Mephistopheles, and draws wine of any predetermined color and taste out of the woodenest things. An author is pronounced brilliant, profound, fascinating, or what not, and is never asked that most important question, the answer to which can alone determine his right to be an author at all,—Do you *mean* anything? No distinction is made between bookwrights who write because they choose, and those who write because they were born to that precise avocation and no other. If a book be merely the safety-valve for that superfluous activity which might have found an equally satisfactory outlet in the manufacture of a shoe, it is no book at all, and no criticism, how liberal soever, can make it anything other than so many pages of printed paper. The truth is, that the phrase liberal criticism is purely a misnomer. There can be no such thing, any more than there can be a liberal inch or a liberal ell. Nor, on the other hand, can there, in strict definition, be such a thing as illiberal criticism. If it incline either way from rigid justice, it is either eulogy or detraction. We might as truly call that a balance where short measure is made full by a thread run through the counter. Criticism is the unbiased application of certain well-defined and self-existent principles of judgment, and the first question to be put to a book is, whether it satisfies any want of the time, or, better still, any want of human nature which knows no time, or whether it were honestly intended so to do. They who cry out for liberal criticism are like those worthy Poundtexts who went about proclaiming the accession of King Jesus when they were really only the unconscious heralds of King Log, they, of course, forming the cabinet. Cromwell saw their drift better than they did themselves, and quietly suppressed them before they had a chance to suppress everything else.

For our own part, we cannot see any use that is to be answered by such books as Tancred. It is as dumb as the poor choked hunchback in the Arabian Nights, when we ask it what its business is. There are no characters in it. There is no dramatic interest, none of plot or incident. Dickens, with his many and egregious faults of style, his mannerisms, and his sometimes intolerable descriptive passages, is yet clearly enough a great genius, a something necessary to the world, and the figures upon his canvas are such as Emerson has aptly termed *representative,* the types of classes, and no truer in London than in Boston. Mr. D'Israeli, when he undertakes to draw a character, sketches some individual whom he happens to like or dislike, and who is no otherwise an individual than by the mere accident of being an actually living person, who has a name on the door in some street or other, who eats, drinks, and like the rest of us is subject to death and bores. For example, we perceive that Mr. Vavasour is intended for Mr. R. M. Milnes, an excellent person and no mean poet, but in no way so peculiar and distinct that this sketch of him presents any definite image, except to those who chance to know the individual intended.

In Tancred there are one or two excellent landscapes, and some detached thoughts worth remembering. There are a vast many girds at Sir Robert Peel, who, after all is said, has shown himself capable of one thing beyond Mr. D'Israeli's reach,—success, which always gives a man some hold or other, however questionable, upon posterity, and arms him in mail of proof against sarcasm. Mr. D'Israeli uses him as a militia company sometimes serve an unpopular politician. He sets up a rude likeness of him for a practising target; but, no matter how many balls may perforate the wooden caricature, its original still walks about unharmed, and with whatever capacity a politician has for enjoying life undiminished. We are introduced to some Arabs who talk very much in the style of Mr. Cooper's red men. It seems to be a peculiarity of savages (if we may say it without derogating from the claims of civilization,) to utter a variety of nothings in a very grave and sententious way. These, at least, are as solemn and as stupid as allegories on the banks of the Nile, or anywhere else. One of them recites a poem which we fancy will never be translated to a place among the Moâllakát. But we cannot undertake to give a sketch of the principal events in Tancred. Such attempts result usually in something like the good monk's epitome of Homer in the *Epistolæ Obscurorum Virorum.* In this particular case, whenever we attempt to call up an individual impression of the book, our memory presents us with nothing but a painfully defiant blur. Moralists tell us, that every man is bound to sustain his share in the weight of the world's sorrows and trials, and we honestly feel as if we had done our part by reading Tancred. If our readers have faithfully got to the end of our article, we cry quits.

"THE NEW TIMON"

"THE NEW TIMON"[1]

FLETCHER of Saltoun's apothegm would hardly answer for our latitude; song has no super-legislative force among us. The walls of one of our great political parties were thought to have risen from their ruins a few years ago,[2] like those of Thebes, to the sound of singing; but this Amphionic mason-work was found not to resist our changeful climate. Our national melodies are of African descent. If our brains are stolen, it will never be through our ears; the Sirens had sung in vain to a Nantucket Ulysses. We remember a nomadic minstrel, a dweller in tents, who picked up a scanty subsistence by singing "Proud Dacre sailed the sea," and "The Hunters *of* Kentucky," on election days, and at Commencements and musters. But he was merely the satellite to a dwarf, and the want of the aspirate betrayed a Transatlantic origin. Moreover, only slender-witted persons were betrayed into the extravagance of the initiatory ninepence, the shrewder citizens contenting themselves with what gratuitous music leaked through the rents in the canvas.

Mr. Barlow, we believe, had a beatific vision of the nine immigrant Muses, somewhere on the top

[1] *The New Timon, a Romance of London.* [By Bulwer-Lytton. —Ed.]

[2] Written in 1847.—Ed.

of the Alleghany mountains. A judicious selection of place;—for only in some such inaccessible spot would they be safe from the constable. Without question, a ship's captain importing nine ladies with so scanty a wardrobe would be compelled to give bonds. With us the band has no chartered sacredness; cotton and the stocks refuse to budge at his vaticinations. The newspapers are our Westminster Abbey, in whose Poets' Corner the fugitive remains of our verse-makers slumber inviolate,—a sacred privacy, uninvaded save by the factory-girl or the seamstress. The price-current is our Paradise of Daintie Devyces; and that necromancer, who might fill his pockets by contracting to bring back Captain Kidd to tell us where he buried treasure, would starve, were he to promise merely

> "To call up him who left half told
> The story of Cambuscan bold."

It is not that we are an antipoetical people. Our surveyors might fix that stigma upon us, by whose means Graylock becomes Saddle-mountain on the maps, and Tahconic is converted from his paganism, and undergoes baptism as Mount Everett. All the world over, the poet is not what he was in ruder times. If he ever unite, as formerly, the bardic and sacerdotal offices, that conjunction forebodes nothing graver than the publication of a new hymn-book. The sanctity of the character is gone; the garret is no safer than the first-floor. Every dun and tipstaff sets at naught the precedent of the great Emathian conqueror. Poetry once concerned itself with the very staple of existence. Now it is a thing apart. The only time we were ever conscious that the Muse did still sometimes cast a halo round every-day life was when we heard the "Village Blacksmith" congratulating himself, that Longfellow had had his smithy "drawed as nateral as a picter."

Many respectable persons are greatly exercised in spirit at the slow growth of what they are pleased to call a national literature. They conjecture of the forms of our art from the shape of our continent, reversing the Platonic method. They deduce a literary from a geographical originality; a new country, therefore new thoughts. A *reductio ad absurdum* would carry this principle to the extent of conforming an author's mind to the house he lived in. These enthusiasts wonder, that our mountains have not yet brought forth a poet, forgetting that a mouse was the result of the only authentic mountainous parturition on record. Others, more hopeful, believe the continent to be at least seven months gone with a portentous minstrel, who, according to the most definite augury we have seen, shall "string" our woods, mountains, lakes, and rivers, and then "wring" from them (no milder term, or less suggestive of the laundry, will serve) notes of "autochthonic significance." We have heard of one author, who thinks it quite needless to be at the pains of a jury of matrons on the subject, as he makes no doubt that the child of Destiny is already born, and that he has discovered in himself the genuine *Terræ Filius.*

Never was there so much debate of a national literature as during the period immediately succeeding our Revolution, and never did the Titan of native song make such efforts to get himself born as then. Hopkinson, Freneau, Paine, and Barlow were the result of that travail. It was not the fault of the country; it was even newer then than now, and its shape (if that was to be effectual in the matter) was identical. Nor was zeal or pains wanting. It is believed that the "Conquest of Canaan" and the "Vision of Columbus" were read by authentic men and women. The same patriotism which refused the tea swallowed the poetry. The same hardy spirit, the same patient endurance, which brought the Pilgrims to Plymouth rock, was not yet gone out of the stock. A nation which had just gone through a seven years' war could undergo a great deal.

But we must come sooner or later to the conclusion, that literature knows no climatic distinctions of that external kind which are presupposed in this clamor for a national literature. The climate in which the mind of an author habitually dwells—whether it be that of Greece, Asia, Italy, Germany, or England—molds the thought and the expression. But that which makes poetry poetry, and not prose, is the same everywhere. The curse of Babel fell not upon the muse. Climate gives inexorable laws to architecture, and all importations from abroad are contraband of nature, sure to be satirized by whatever is native to the soil. There is but one sky of song, and the growth of the tropics will bear the open air of the pole. For man is the archetype of poetry. Its measure and proportion, as Vitruvius reports of the Doric pillar, are borrowed of him. Natural scenery has little hand in it, national peculiarities none at all. Not Simoïs or Scamander, but Helen, Priam, Andromache, give divinity to the tale of Troy. Dante's Italicism is his lame foot. Shakspeare would fare ill, were we to put him upon proof of his Englishry. So homogeneous is the structure of the mind, that Sir William Jones conceived Odin and Fo to be identical.

There is no fear but we shall have a national literature soon enough. Meanwhile, we may be sure that all attempts at the forcible manufacture of such a product (especially out of physical elements) will be as fruitless as the *opus magnum* of the alchemists. The cunning of man can only adroitly combine the materials lying ready to his hand. It has never yet compassed the creation of any seed, be it never so small. As a nation, we are yet too full of hurry and bustle. The perfectly balanced tree can grow only in the wind-bound shelter of the valley. Our national eagerness for immediate results infests our literature. We wish to taste the fruit of our culture, and as yet plant not that slower growth which ripens for posterity. The mental characteristic of the pioneer has become engrained in us, outliving the necessity which begot it. Everywhere the blackened stumps of the clearing jut out like rocks amid the yellow waves of our harvest. We have not learned to wait; our chief aim is to produce, and we are more careful of quantity than quality. We cannot bring ourselves to pinch off a part of the green fruit, that the ripe may be more perfect. To be left behind is the opprobrium; we desire an immediate effect. Hence, a large part of that mental energy, which would else find its natural bent in literary labor, turns to the lecture-room or the caucus, or mounts that ready-made rostrum of demagogues, the stump. If any man think he has an errand for the general ear, he runs at full speed with it, and delivers such fragments as he has breath left to utter. If we adopt a Coptic emblem, and paste it on the front of our pine-granite propylæa, it must have wings, implying speed. That symbol of wiser meaning, with finger upon lip, is not for us. We break our eggs, rather than await the antiquated process of incubation. We pull up what we have planted, to see if it have taken root. We fell the primeval forest, and thrust into the ground a row of bean-poles for shade. We cannot spare the time to sleep upon anything; we must be through by daylight. Our boys debate the tariff and the war. Scarce yet beyond the lacteal stage, they leave hoop, and ball, and taw, to discuss the tea and coffee tax.

We find talk cheaper than writing, and both easier than thinking. We talk everlastingly; our magazines are nothing but talk, and that of a flaccid and Polonian fibre. The Spartans banished the unfortunate man who boasted that he could talk all day. With us he has been sure of Congress or the Cabinet. No petty African king is fonder of palaver than the sovereign people. Our national bird is of no kin to the falcon of the Persian poet, whose taciturnity made him of more esteem than the nightingale. We are always in haste; we build a railroad from the cradle to the grave. Our children cannot spare time to learn spelling; they must take the short cut of phonography. In architecture, we cannot abide the slow teaching of the fitness of things; we parody the sacred growth of ages with our inch-board fragilities,

> "Their rafters sprouting on the shady side,"

and every village boasts its *papier-machè* cathedral. Our railroad-cars are our best effort in this kind yet,—the emblems of hurry. The magnetic telegraph is of our invention, a message upon which, traveling westward, outstrips Time himself. The national trait is aptly symbolized by a gentleman we know of, who has erected his own funeral monument (what a titbit for honest old Weever!) and inscribed upon it an epitaph of his own composing, leaving vacant only the date of his demise. This is to be beforehand with Death himself. We remember only the *occasio celeris* and not the *ars longa* of the adage. Hence a thousand sciolists for one scholar, a hundred improvisators for one poet. Everything with us ripens so rapidly, that nothing of ours seems very old but our boys.

A sandy diffuseness of style among our speakers and writers is the result of this hurry. We try to grasp a substantial handful here and there, and it runs through our fingers. How our legislators contrive to sit out each other's speeches we could never conceive. Who reads those interminable debates is a question of harder solution than what song the Sirens sang. In our callower years, we sit down beside them, like the clown at the river's edge. But we soon learn the *labitur et labetur*. Providence, which has made nothing that is not food for something else, has doubtless so constituted some systems as that they can devour and digest these. The constituency of Buncombe, if it find time to read all that is addressed to it, must be endowed with an unmatched longevity. It must be a community of oldest inhabitants. Yet, with all this tendency to prosing, we love concentration, epigrammatic brevity, antithesis. Hence the potency of phrases among us; a nimble phrase in a trice trips up our judgment; "masterly inactivity," "conquering a peace," "our country right or wrong," and the like. Talleyrand's plan for settling the Restoration on a firm basis would have done for us:—"C'est bien, c'est très bien, et tout ce qu'il faut maintenant, ce sont les feux d'artifice *et un bon mot pour le peuple*."

Under such circumstances, we need hardly expect a sudden crop of epics. We must have something that we can bolt. And we need not trouble ourselves about the form or the growth of our literature. The law of demand and supply is as inexorable here as in every thing else. The forcing system, we may be sure, is out of place. Art cannot make heartwood under glass. Above all, let not our young authors be seduced into the belief, that there can be any nationality in the great leading ideas of art. The mind has one shape in the Esquimaux and the Anglo-Saxon, and that shape it will strive to impress on its creations. If we evaporate all that is watery, and the mere work of absorption, in the mythologies and early histories of the different races of men, we shall find one invariable residuum at bottom. The legendary age of Greece may find a parallel in our own recent history, and "Old Put," the wolf-killer, at whose door all the unfathered *derring-does* of the time are laid, is no mean Yankee translation of Theseus. Doubtless, a freer and more untrammeled spirit will be the general characteristic of our literature, and it is to be hoped that it will get its form and pressure before our social life begins (as it inevitably must) to fence itself from the approaches of license behind a stricter and more rigid conventionality. Where external distinctions are wanting, men intrench themselves the more deeply in forms. When this reaction makes itself felt in our literature, let us hope to find the works of our authors as conscientious in finish, as they should be bold in design and outline. As for expecting that our mountains and lakes and forests should inoculate our literature with their idiosyncrasies, we may as reasonably look to find the mental results of our corduroy roads there, a speculation which might confirm itself by certain metres we have lately been favored with by our poets. The "surface of the country," of which we used to read so much in our geographies, never made and never marred a poet. There are mountains as good as Chimborazo and Popocatapetl in the poet's mind. Were Skiddaw and Ben Lomond the lay-figures from which Bunyan painted his Delectable Mountains? Or was the dead marsh-level of parts of the Excursion an infection from those hills among which Wordsworth has spent his life? Shakspeare has done better than travel in Egypt when he said,—

> "Ye pyramids, built up with newer might,
> To me are nothing novel, nothing strange;
> *Ye are but dressings of a former sight.*"

Hitherto our literature has been chiefly imitative and artificial; we have found no better names for our authors than the American Scott, the American Mrs. Hemans, the American Wordsworth. There is nothing to fear from too great license as yet. At present, every English author can see a distorted reflection of himself here,—a something like the eidolons of the Homeric Hades, not ghosts precisely, but unsubstantial counterparts. He finds himself come round again, the Atlantic Ocean taking the function of the Platonic year. Our authors are the best critics of their brethren (or parents) on the other side of the water, catching as they do only what is exaggerated in them. We are in need of a

Others commend it on the score of its being easily comprehensible. Others again are charmed with what they esteem the grace, precision, and finish of its metre.

It is unquestionably the prime merit of style, that it conveys the author's ideas exactly and clearly. But after all, the ideas to be conveyed are of more importance than the vehicle, and it is one thing to see distinctly what they are, and another to comprehend them. Undoubtedly the first requisite is that they be worth comprehending. Once establish the principle, that easiness of comprehension is the chief merit in literature, and the lowest order of minds will legislate for the exercise of that faculty which should give law to the highest. Every new book would come to us with the ambiguous compliment, that it was adapted to the meanest capacity. We have never been able to appreciate with any tolerable distinctness the grounds of that complacent superiority implied in the confession of not being able to understand an author, though we have frequently seen airs assumed on the strength of that acknowledged incapacity. One has a vision of the lame, halt, and blind dropping compassionate fourpences into the hats of their unmutilated fellow-citizens. Apelles judged rightly in pronouncing Alexander's horse a better critic than his master. The equine was more liberal than the imperial appreciation.

The merit of Pope is wholly of the intellect. There is nothing in him of that finer instinct which characterizes all those who, by universal consent, have been allowed as great poets, and have received the laurel from posterity. His instinct is rather that of a man of taste than of genius. In reading Shakspeare, we do not concern ourselves as to the particular shape which his thoughts assume. That is wholly a secondary affair. We should as soon think of criticizing the peculiar form of a tree or a fern. Though we may not be able to codify the law which governs them, we cannot escape a feeling of the harmony and fitness resulting from an obedience to that law. There is a necessity for their being of that precise mold, and no other, which peremptorily overrules all cavil. With Pope, on the contrary, the form is what first demands notice. It is here that the poet has put forth his power and displayed his skill. He makes verses by a voluntary exercise of the intellect, rather than from the overflow of the creative power. We feel that he had his choice between several forms of expression, and was not necessarily constrained to the one he has selected. His verses please us, as any display of mental skill and vigor never fails to do. The pleasure he gives us is precisely similar to that we derive from reading the Spectator, and is in both cases the result of identical causes. His apothegms are wholly of the intellect, and that, too, of the intellect applied to the analysis of artificial life. He does not, according to Bacon's definition of poetry, "conform the shows of things to the desires of the soul." Yet he dwells in the shows of things rather literary declaration of independence; our literature should no longer be colonial.

Let us not be understood as chiming in with that foolish cry of the day, that authors should not profit by example and precedent,—a cry which generally originates with some hardy imitator, the "stop thief!" with which he would fain distract attention from himself. It is the tower-stamp of an original mind, that it gives an awakening impulse to other original minds. Memory was the mother of the Muses. Montaigne says, "In my country, when they would decipher a man that has no sense, they say such a one has no memory." But to imitate the works of another is not to profit by them. It is making them our dungeon. It is better to smell of the lamp than of the library. Yet the most original writers have begun in some sort as imitators, and necessarily so. They must first learn to speak by watching the lips and practising the tones of others. This once acquired, the native force within masters and molds the instrument. Shakspeare's early poems have the trick and accent of Spenser. Milton's Comus was written with a quill from the Swan of Avon's wing, dipped in Jonson's ink. But even the imitations of an original mind give no small oracle of originality. The copyist mimics mannerisms only. Like Crashaw's minstrel,

> "From this to that, from that to this, he flies."

The original mind is always consistent with itself. Michel Angelo, cramped by the peculiar shape of a piece of marble which another sculptor had roughed out for a conception of his own, conquered something characteristic out of that very restraint, and the finished statue proclaimed its author. The poet, like the sculptor, works in one material, and there, in the formless quarry of the language, lie the divine shapes of gods and heroes awaiting the master's evocation.

The republication of a poem which has made a sensation in England is not without its importance to us. We read of an ancient nation who, every New Year, made clean hearths, and then rekindled them with fire sent round by their king for that end. A rite not unlike this in form, though widely different in meaning, is still maintained by many of our authors. So soon as a new light makes its appearance in England, every native rushlight is ceremoniously extinguished, and the smoking wick set once more ablaze by the stolen touch of that more prosperous foreign flame. From the avatar of this Christmas we cannot remotely conjecture in what shape an author shall choose to appear at the next. But the book, which we have made the text of our somewhat erratic discourse, is not only worthy of notice, inasmuch as it may serve as a model, but still more from its own intrinsic merits, and because it is a strong protest against the form and spirit of the poetry now in vogue. It once more unburies the hatchet of the ancient feud between what are called the "natural" and "artificial" schools.

The dispute in this case, as in most others, has

concerned itself chiefly about words. An exact definition of the terms used by the contending parties would have been the best flag of truce. Grant the claims of the disciples of Pope, and you blot out at once the writings of the greatest poets that ever lived. Grant those of the opposite party, and you deny to Pope any merit whatever. The cardinal point of the whole quarrel lies in the meaning attached to the single word *poet.* The most potent champion of *Popery* in our day gave by his practice the direct lie to his assumed theory. The Age of Bronze, the only poem which he wrote professedly upon this model, is unreadable from sheer dullness. His prose letters in the Bowles controversy were far more in Pope's vein and spirit.

The author of the New Timon avows himself a follower of Pope. We shall by-and-by have occasion to try him by his own standard. In the meantime, we shall barely remark, that his allusions to Wordsworth, Tennyson, and Keats are presumptuous and in bad taste. The fact that he misspells the name of one of these poets argues either a very petty affectation, or a shameful unfamiliarity with what he pretends to criticize.

The truth is, that Pope's merit lies in the concinnity and transparency of his style. It is this, rather than the sentiment, which charms. Thousands of readers find no want of orthodoxy in the Essay on Man, who would recoil in horror from the rough draught of Bolingbroke, on which it was based. Fancy, purity of diction, conciseness, unfailing wit, all these are Pope's, and they have given him immortality. But these are not essentially the attributes of a poet. In imagination, the crowning faculty of the poet, nay, the one quality which emphatically distinguishes him as such, Pope is wanting. A single example of the pure exercise of this faculty is not to be found in his works.

A profusion of ignorance and bad temper have been lavished on this topic. Had the controversy been understandingly carried on, there would have been no occasion for ill-feeling. One chief blunder has been the defining of authors as belonging to a certain school because they happened to be addicted to the use of a measure consisting of a certain number of feet, yet not the less variable on that account. Dryden, Pope, and Goldsmith are commonly named together,—authors as dissimilar as Chaucer and Racine. Crabbe, Campbell, and Rogers have all three used the same measure, yet are wholly unlike each other and unlike their three predecessors above named. Byron, who also used the "English Heroic" (as it is commonly called) in the Corsair and some other poems, presents still another totally distinct variety.

What, then, is the secret of that predilection in the minds of many to that kind of writing which is rather vaguely defined to be "of the Pope school?" Many, no doubt, adhere to it on the ground of its age and respectability,—a prejudice which Pope himself has admirably satirized.

Others commend it on the score of its being easily comprehensible. Others again are charmed with what they esteem the grace, precision, and finish of its metre.

It is unquestionably the prime merit of style, that it conveys the author's ideas exactly and clearly. But after all, the ideas to be conveyed are of more importance than the vehicle, and it is one thing to see distinctly what they are, and another to comprehend them. Undoubtedly the first requisite is that they be worth comprehending. Once establish the principle, that easiness of comprehension is the chief merit in literature, and the lowest order of minds will legislate for the exercise of that faculty which should give law to the highest. Every new book would come to us with the ambiguous compliment, that it was adapted to the meanest capacity. We have never been able to appreciate with any tolerable distinctness the grounds of that complacent superiority implied in the confession of not being able to understand an author, though we have frequently seen airs assumed on the strength of that acknowledged incapacity. One has a vision of the lame, halt, and blind dropping compassionate fourpences into the hats of their unmutilated fellow-citizens. Apelles judged rightly in pronouncing Alexander's horse a better critic than his master. The equine was more liberal than the imperial appreciation.

The merit of Pope is wholly of the intellect. There is nothing in him of that finer instinct which characterizes all those who, by universal consent, have been allowed as great poets, and have received the laurel from posterity. His instinct is rather that of a man of taste than of genius. In reading Shakspeare, we do not concern ourselves as to the particular shape which his thoughts assume. That is wholly a secondary affair. We should as soon think of criticizing the peculiar form of a tree or a fern. Though we may not be able to codify the law which governs them, we cannot escape a feeling of the harmony and fitness resulting from an obedience to that law. There is a necessity for their being of that precise mold, and no other, which peremptorily overrules all cavil. With Pope, on the contrary, the form is what first demands notice. It is here that the poet has put forth his power and displayed his skill. He makes verses by a voluntary exercise of the intellect, rather than from the overflow of the creative power. We feel that he had his choice between several forms of expression, and was not necessarily constrained to the one he has selected. His verses please us, as any display of mental skill and vigor never fails to do. The pleasure he gives us is precisely similar to that we derive from reading the Spectator, and is in both cases the result of identical causes. His apothegms are wholly of the intellect, and that, too, of the intellect applied to the analysis of artificial life. He does not, according to Bacon's definition of poetry, "conform the shows of things to the desires of the soul." Yet he dwells in the shows of things rather than in the substances, and conforms them, sometimes, despotically, to the necessities of his satire. He jeers and flouts the artificial life which he sees. He mocks at it, as Lucian derided Zeus,—an atheist to the gods of the day, with no settled belief in any higher gods. He does not confute the artificial by comparison with any abiding real. He impales all contemporary littlenesses upon the sharp needles of his wit, and in his poems, as in an entomological cabinet, we see preserved all the ugly insects of his day. He does not tacitly rebuke meanness by looking over it to the image of a perennial magnanimity. He does not say sternly, "Get thee behind me, Satan!" but mischievously affixes a stinging epigram to horns, hoof, and tail, and sends Beelzebub away ridiculous. His inkstand was his arsenal, but it was not his to use it in Luther's hearty catapultic fashion.

We do not so much commend the New Timon, then, as being a return to purer models, but as a protest against the excesses into which the prevailing school had degenerated. Latterly, poetry seems to have deserted the strong and palpable motions of the common heart, and to have devoted itself to the ecstatic exploration of solitary nerves,—the less tangible, the better. The broad view attainable from those two peaks of Parnassus, which Sir John Denham sensibly defined to be "Nature and Skill," seems to be well-nigh neglected. Our young poets, instead of that healthy glow of cheek earned only by conversation with the robust air of the summit, and the labor incident to the rugged ascent, seem to value themselves upon their paleness, and to think him the better man who has spent most time in peering dizzily down the dark rifts and chasms round the base of the mountain, or in gazing into the potential millstones of its solid rock. The frailer the tissue of the feeling, the greater the merit in tracing it to its extremes,—a spiderlike accomplishment at best. Their philosophy (if we call that so which they esteem as such, and which is certainly nothing else) stands in grave need of Philotas's leaden soles. One might almost expect to see them blown out of existence by the incautious puffs of their own publisher or clique. The farther the poet can put himself out of the common, the more admirable is he. The reflections of Perillus in his bull, of Regulus in his hogshead, or of Clarence in his malmsey-butt, would furnish an ample stock in trade to any young poet. Or a nearer approach to nature and the interests of every-day life might be found in the situation of Terance McHugh, buried alive at the bottom of a well, and so finding it to be the residence of at least one unquestionable verity.

Mystery, too, has become a great staple with our poets. Everything must be accounted for by something more unaccountable. Grandgousier's simple and pious theory to explain the goodliness of Friar John's nose would hardly pass muster now. The "mystery of our being" has become a favorite object of contemplation. Egoism has been erected into a system of theology. Self has been deified like the Egyptian onion,—

> "Nascuntur in hortis
> Numina."

Poets used to look before and after. Now, their eyes are turned wholly inward, and ordinarily with as useful result as was attained by the Brahmin who spent five years in the beatific inspection of his own navel. Instead of poems, we have lectures on the morbid anatomy of self. Nature herself must subscribe their platform of doctrine, and that not "for substance, scope, and aim," but without qualification. If they turn their eyes outward for a moment, they behold in the landscape only a smaller image of themselves. The mountain becomes a granite Mr. Smith, and the ocean (leaving out the salt) a watery Mr. Brown, —in other words a Mr. Brown with the milky particles of his composition deducted. A new *systema mundi* is constructed, with the individual idiosyncrasy of the poet for its base. And, to prolong the delight of swallowing all this sublime mystification, enraptured simplicity prays fervently, with the old epicure, for the neck of a crane. Fortunately, that of a goose will suffice.

Nor has our mother tongue been safe from the experimental incursions of these philosophers. They have plunged so deeply into the well of English undefiled as to bring up the mud from the bottom. This they call "Saxon," and infuse portions of it into their productions, deepening the turbid obscurity. Strange virtues have been discovered in compound words, and the greater the incongruity of the mixture, the more potent the conjuration. Phrases, simple or unmeaning enough in themselves, acquire force and become mystical by repetition, like the three *Iods* of the Cabbalists, or the Κόγξ Ὄμπαξ of the Eleusinian mysteries. Straightforwardness has become a prose virtue. The poet wanders about his subject, looks for it where he knows it is not, and avoids looking where he knows it is, like a child playing at hide-and-seek, who, to lengthen the pleasure of the hunt, peeps cautiously into keyholes and every other impossible place, leaving to the last the table, under which lurks, with ostrich-like obviousness, the object of his search. It had been fortunate for Columbus, could he have recruited his crews with such minstrels, whose only mutiny would have been at the finding of the expected continent. We have seen the translation of a Hindoo deed which affords an exact parallel to such poetry. It begins with a general history of India, diverges into a system of theology, exhausts all the grantor's knowledge of natural history and astronomy, relates a few fables on different subjects, throws in a confused mass of compound words (one of them containing one hundred and fifty-two syllables), and finally reveals the object of this ponderous legal machine in a postscript of six lines conveying an acre or two of land.

The New Timon, if not the exact reverse of all

this, is at least a resolute attempt in the opposite direction. We do not believe it possible to revive the style of Pope. It was a true mirror of its own age, but it would imperfectly reflect ours. Its very truth then would make it false now. The *petere fontes* points to other springs than these. Much less do we believe in confining literature to the strait channel of any one period. That is surely a very jejune kind of conservatism, which, with the Athenian Ephorus, would cut every new string added to the lyre. The critics have too often assumed the office of Ephorus in our commonwealth of letters, and have unfortunately become impressed with the notion, that this chordisection is the chief part of their official duty. As Selden said that equity was measured by the length of my Lord Chancellor's foot for the time being, so has judgment in these cases been too often meted, if not by the length, at least by the susceptibility, of my Lord Ephorus's ear. If every Phrynio had been thus dealt with, the lyre would never have lost that pristine simplicity and compactness, and that facility at making itself understood, which characterized it when it was a plain tortoise-shell, ere idle Hermes had embarrassed and perplexed it with a single string.

The author is a professed disciple of Pope, but he is wanting in the vivid common-sense, the crystal terseness, and the epigrammatic point of his original. Moreover, he is something of a "snob." His foundling Lucy must turn out to be an earl's daughter; his Hindoo Timon must be a nabob.

It is clear that he reverences those very artificial distinctions which he professes to scorn. So much contempt could not be lavished on what was insignificant. Himself the child of a highly artificial state of society, there seems to be something unfilial and against nature in his assaults upon it. His New Timon is made a Timon by the very things which he affects to despise. Pope was quite superior to so subaltern a feeling.

The plot of the story is not much to our taste. Morvale, the hero, is the son of a half-Hindoo father and an English mother. The mother, left a widow,

"Loathed the dark pledge the abhorred nuptials bore;
Yet young, her face more genial wedlock won,
And one bright daughter made more loathed the son.
Widowed anew, for London's native air
And two tall footmen sighed the jointured fair;
Wealth hers, why longer from its use exiled?
She fled the land and the abandoned child."

In the meanwhile, a rich friend of Morvale's father opportunely dies, leaving his immense wealth to the son. This self-devotion on the part of the very rich is happily universal in the Utopia of the novel and the melodrama. We are thus introduced to Mr. Morvale.

"They sought and found the unsuspecting heir
Couched in the shade that neared the tiger's lair,
His gun beside, the jungle round him,—wild,
Lawless, and fierce as Hagar's wandering child:—
To this fresh nature the sleek life deceased
Left the bright plunder of the ravaged East.

Much wealth brings want,—that hunger of the heart
Which comes when Nature man deserts for Art:
His northern blood, his English name, create
Strife in the soul till then resigned to fate;
The social world, with blander falsehood graced,
Smiles on his hopes and lures him from the waste.
Alas! the taint that sunburnt brow bespeaks
Divides the Half-Caste from the world he seeks;
In him proud Europe sees the Paria's birth,
And haughty Juno spurns his barren hearth.
Half heathen and half savage,—all estranged
Amidst his kind, the Ishmael roved unchanged."

We do not profess to be in Juno's confidence, but, unless she is greatly belied, she is not in the habit of examining closely the complexion of a millionaire. Wealth produces a marvelous change in Morvale, at least. He now travels, converses much with books and men, drinks life at once to the dregs (the favorite beverage of heroes), and becomes one of those profoundly learned men of the world, more familiar to the patrons of circulating libraries than to any other class in society. These singular beings are the antithesis of ordinary natures. They are incarnate contradictions. Fire and gunpowder in them meet on amicable terms. A liberal course of dissipation fulfils more than the functions of a university. In the society of opera-girls, they learn to be fastidious in women; in that of *roués,* they exhaust the arts and sciences. We do not say that Morvale is precisely one of these, but we have hints, every here and there, of something like it. We would only warn him from ground sacred to Madame Tussaud and the melodrama.

Morvale, having run round the elevated circle of the passions, subsides to a less heroic, but much more respectable, stratum of existence. His feelings as a son and brother revive. He accordingly, we are told, "*searched* his mother," a perilous infringement of orthoëpy, or of the rights of the subject, if done without a justice's warrant. He does not find her, however, she being probably one of those highly artificial characters who never carry themselves about with them. She avoids him

> "Till Death approached, and Conscience, that sad star,
> That heralds Night, and plays but on the bar
> Of the Eternal Gate,—laid bare the crime."

She leaves her daughter Calantha to his fraternal care. The brother and sister go to housekeeping together in the magnificent isolation of London. But though there is enough affection, there is little confidence, between them. A secret melancholy, the origin of which Morvale tries in vain to discover, preys upon the spirits of Calantha,—the old "worm i' the bud." Morvale, in one of his walks, encounters an orphan, Lucy, whom he brings home with him, and makes an inmate of his house, where, in good time, a passion springs up between them.

One of Morvale's friends—and it is a little singular, that notwithstanding the barrier of his Hindoo blood, he moves in the most fashionable society—is Lord Arden, a *blasé* like himself, who one day, while they are riding together, relates his own history. Whatever fault we may find with our author's plot, we cannot but approve his method of unfolding it. He tells his stories admirably, and interests us in spite of ourselves. But we must be careful that this does not interfere with our judgment of him as a poet. An author may be a very good story-teller, and a very bad poet. The character of Arden is well conceived. Indeed, it is by far the best in the book. The story had been truer to nature, if he, who had been through life brought into contact with the hollownesses of society, had become the Timon instead of Morvale. A man of the world, and selfish (if we may say so) rather on æsthetic grounds than by nature, he falls in love, while yet quite young, with Mary, the daughter of a poor country curate. Arden is one of the presumptive heirs to an earldom, the present earl being his uncle, and a cunning Scot has barnacled himself to the prosperous ship of his fortunes. Through him, Arden contrives an elopement and clandestine marriage. The Scot, however, knowing that Arden's uncle, the earl, looked upon a wife as merely one round in the ladder of preferment, and would infallibly withdraw his patronage, if he discovered such a mark of unthrift in his nephew as disinterested love, has the ceremony performed by a mock priest. Mary's father, finding the marriage to be a sham, dies broken-hearted, and Mary herself, compelled to believe herself betrayed, leaves her home and wanders no one knows whither. Arden, meanwhile, ignorant of all this, has gone on a foreign embassy. On his return, he becomes aware of the deceit practised upon him in regard to the marriage, but seeks Mary in vain. After the lapse of some years, he meets a lady in Italy, to whom he becomes betrothed. The day for the wedding is already fixed, when he receives letters from England, giving a hope that Mary's hiding-place may be found. Leaving his betrothed with a hasty and unintelligible explanation, he hastens home, where his search is again unsuccessful. So far Arden is his own biographer.

After a time, Morvale, by means of a miniature worn by Lucy, discovers that she is the daughter of Arden and Mary. He is about to send for Arden to inform him of this fact, when he makes the additional discovery, that Calantha is the nameless lady to whom his friend had been betrothed in Italy, and that his desertion of her was the occasion of that profound melancholy which was gradually killing her. He sends for Arden, and receives him by the death-bed of Calantha. His Indian nature thirsts for revenge, and, after making known his last discovery to the man whom he now considers his deadliest foe, draws a dagger, but is arrested in the act of striking by the entrance of Lucy, who throws herself between them. The relationship between Lucy and Arden is revealed, and she goes home with her father. Morvale, still struggling with his savage thirst for vengeance, wanders over the country on foot, and at last meets with an old man who converts him to Christianity. A chance occurring, he saves Arden from drowning, but leaves him before he has recovered his consciousness, though not before he has been seen and recognized by Lucy. Arden at length dies. By an informality in his will, Lucy is disinherited, and at this juncture Morvale returns in season to have the story end canonically with a wedding.

Our brief sketch does no kind of justice, of course, to the narrative skill of the author, which is, we are inclined to think, his strong point. But the comparative anatomist will see at a glance, that the skeleton is in many parts inconsistent with itself. Even granting (a large concession), that the hereditary savage in Morvale should have withstood all the refining influences of a high artificial culture, and the Mephistophelic polish acquired by attrition with the world, there is still a geographical blunder in the character. It is far less in accordance with what we know of the mild nature of the Hindoo, than with the less tractable idiosyncrasy of our American Indian, which takes the color of the white man's civilization only as a paint through which the Maker's original red shows itself at the first opportunity. But after making this allowance, we feel that the author has not used the character to the best advantage. This fresh, unfettered nature might have been brought into fine contrast with Arden, the artificial product of the club and the saloon. Indeed, this seems to have been the author's original design, but in point of fact there is little substantial difference between the two characters as they are exhibited to us in the narrative, and they might change places without any great shock to the reader's sense of fitness.[2] Our author *makes up* his characters. His mind is not of that creative quality which holds the elements of different characters, as it were, in solution, allowing each to absorb only that which is congenial to itself, by a kind of elective affinity. The only savage propensity of Morvale's nature which is brought to bear upon the story is the sentiment of revenge, and for this the motive is not sufficient. Why should Morvale wish, or how could he expect, that Arden should have committed what would have been at least moral bigamy by marrying Calantha? If not, what injury was there to avenge? The story, in fact, ends with Arden's discovery of his daughter; the whole of Morvale's conduct after this event seems to be an unnatural excrescence. The author may plead that he intended to convey a moral; but the moral of a story should always be infused into it, or rather should exhale out of every part of it, like the odor of a flower. It is but an incumbrance, when wafered on. Besides, the means by which he manages the conversion of his hero are ludicrously insufficient to the end. If Horace's rule be true, that a god must not be

[2] In his tragedy of "Luria," Mr. Browning has finally worked out an idea similar in kind, though with tragic, and not satirical, contrast. We are glad to recognize in the last work of this very promising dramatist a more assured touch, and a chastened, though by no means diminished, vigor and originality.

brought in unless the knot refuses to be unloosed by simpler means, then it follows, *a fortiori,* that, when brought, the god should be competent to the task in hand. It is absurd that Morvale, after holding out so long against more natural inducements, should be converted at last by a very prosy sermon from an old man whom he meets under a hedge, and whom he would have been much more likely to consider a bore than an apostle. The author should have remembered his master Pope's criticism upon Milton. It would have been much more to the purpose, had Morvale been regenerated by his love for Lucy. As the *dénouement* is managed, we feel very much as when we first discovered that the red man of our boyish imagination, the one hero of Cooper under a dozen aliases,

> "The stoic of the woods, the man without a fear,"

was powerless to resist the persuasion of a string of glass beads.

We will now proceed to extract some of the passages which have struck us most favorably in reading the book, and which give a fair idea of the author's manner and spirit. In the first part of the poem there are a few sketches of well-known public characters, which, as they are complete in themselves, and have no connection with the story, we will quote first. They do not assume to be complete full-lengths, but must be understood as hit off with a pencil on the crown of a hat. We omit that of Sir Robert Peel, who seems to have puzzled our author, and come to the Duke of Wellington.

"Next, with loose rein and careless canter view
Our man of men, the Prince of Waterloo;
O'er the firm brow the hat as firmly prest,
The firm shape rigid in the button'd vest;
Within—the iron which the fire has proved,
And the close Sparta of a mind unmoved!
Not his the wealth to some large natures lent,
Divinely lavish, even where misspent,
That liberal sunshine of exuberant soul,
Thought, sense, affection, warming up the whole;
The heat and affluence of a genial power,
Rank in the weed as vivid in the flower;
Hush'd at command his veriest passions halt,
Drill'd is each virtue, disciplined each fault;
Warm if his blood—he reasons while he glows,
Admits the pleasure—ne'er the folly knows;
If for our Mars his snare had Vulcan set,
He had won the Venus, but escaped the net;
His eye ne'er wrong if circumscribed the sight,
Widen the prospect and it ne'er is right,
Seen through the telescope of habit still,
States seem a camp, and all the world—a drill!"

O'Connell next passes across our magic-lantern.

"But who, scarce less by every gazer eyed,
Walks yonder, swinging with a stalwart stride?
With that vast bulk of chest and limb assign'd
So oft to men who subjugate their kind;
So sturdy Cromwell push'd broad-shoulder'd on;
So burly Luther breasted Babylon;
So brawny Cleon bawl'd his Agora down;
And large-limb'd Mahmoud clutch'd a Prophet's crown!

"Ay, mark him well! the schemer's subtle eye,
The stage-mime's plastic lip your search defy—
He, like Lysander, never deems it sin
To eke the lion's with the fox's skin;
Vain every mesh this Proteus to enthrall,
He breaks no statute, and he creeps through all;
First to the mass that valiant truth to tell,
'Rebellion's art is never to rebel,—
Elude all danger, but defy all laws,'—
He stands himself the Safe Sublime he draws!
In him behold all contrasts which belong
To minds abased, but passions rous'd, by wrong;
The blood all fervor, and the brain all guile,—
The patriot's bluntness, and the bondsman's wile."

The drawing of the present premier is still more happily touched.

"Next cool, and all unconscious of reproach,
Comes the calm 'Johnny who upset the coach.'
How formed to lead, if not too proud to please,—
His frame would fire you, but his manners freeze.
Like or dislike, he does not care a jot;
He wants your vote, but your affections not;
Yet human hearts need sun, as well as oats,—
So cold a climate plays the deuce with votes.—
And while its doctrines ripen day by day,
His frost-nipp'd party pines itself away;—
From the starved wretch its own loved child we steal—
And 'Free Trade' chirrups on the lap of Peel!—
But see our statesman when the steam is on,
And languid Johnny glows to glorious John!
When Hampden's thought, by Falkland's muses drest,
Lights the pale cheek, and swells the generous breast;
When the pent heat expands the quickening soul,—
And foremost in the race the wheels of genius roll!"

It is impossible to do justice to the narrative parts of the poem by means of detached passages. We shall glean a descriptive passage here and there, as a fairer course toward the author, these being at least complete in themselves. The following verses, conveying the feelings suggested by night in London, are striking.

"The Hours steal on—and o'er the unquiet might
Of the great Babel—reigns, dishallowed, Night!
Not, as o'er Nature's world, She comes, to keep
Beneath the stars her solemn tryst with Sleep,
When move the twin-born Genii side by side,
And steal from earth its demons where they glide;
Lull'd the spent Toil—seal'd Sorrow's heavy eyes,
And dreams restore the dews of Paradise;
But Night, discrown'd and sever'd from her twin,
No pause for Travail, no repose for Sin,
Vex'd by one chafed rebellion to her sway,
Flits o'er the lamp-lit streets—a phantom-day!"

Here are a pair of out-of-doors scenes. The first is contained in a very few lines, but it is natural and touching. Arden has returned to England, and is seeking Mary at her old home.

"Behold her home once more!
Her home! a desert!—still, though rank and wild,
On the rank grass the headless floweret smiled;
Still by the porch you heard the ungrateful bee,
Still brawled the brooklet's unremembering glee."

The other is an autumnal landscape. But it must be observed that the author never paints directly from nature, but from the reflection of her in his own mind.

"Now Autumn closes on the fading year,
The chill wind moaneth through the woodlands sere;
At morn the mists lie mournful on the hill,—
The hum of summer's populace is still!
Hush'd the rife herbage, mute the choral tree,
The blithe cicala and the murmuring bee;
The plashing reed, the furrow on the glass
Of the calm wave, as by the bank you pass
Scaring the glistening trout,—delight no more;
The god of fields is dead—Pan's lusty reign is o'er!
Solemn and earnest—yet to holier eyes
Not void of glory, arch the sober'd skies
Above the serious earth!—e'en as the age
When fades the sunlight from the poet's page,
When all Creation is no longer rife,
As Jove's lost creed, with deity and life—
And where Apollo hymn'd, where Venus smil'd;
Where laugh'd from every rose the Paphian child;
Where in each wave the wanton nymph was seen;
Where in each moonbeam shone Endymion's queen;
Where in each laurel, from the eternal bough
Daphne wreathed chaplets for a dreamy brow;
To the wreck'd thrones of the departed creeds
A solemn Faith, a lonely God succeeds;
And o'er the earthen altars of our youth,
Reigns, 'mid a silence disenchanted,—Truth!"

The following night-scene is perhaps the best of its kind in the whole book. The images are all in keeping (a rare thing with our author), and the expression, especially in the verse we have italicized, condensed and energetic.

"'Tis night,—a night by fits, now foul, now fair,
As speed the cloud-wracks through the gusty air:
At times the wild blast dies—and fair and far,
Through chasms of cloud, looks down the solemn star—

Or the majestic moon;—as watchfires mark
Some sleeping War dim-tented in the dark;
Or as, through antique Chaos and the storm
Of Matter, whirl'd and writhing into form
Pale angels peer'd!
"Anon, from brief repose
The winds leap forth, the cloven deeps reclose;
Mass upon mass the hurtling vapors driven,
And one huge blackness walls the earth from heaven!"

As we have said above, narrative seems the author's true sphere. His reflections are often commonplace, sometimes puerile, and display more knowledge of society than of man. Often a thought slender in itself is invested with a burly air by means of initial capitals. But when he has a story to tell, he is in his native element. He never flags, his versification becomes bolder and more sustained, the transitions are rapid and fluent, and incident follows incident without confusion and with a culminating interest.

The author of the New Timon might have studied Pope to more purpose than he has done. He is often exceedingly obscure. *Brevis esse laborat, obscurus fit.* There are passages in the poem which have defied our utmost capacity of penetration. Nor is his use of language always correct. His metaphors are frequently confused, as, for instance:—

"From the way-side yon drooping flower I bore;
Warm'd at my heart, its root grew to the core."

A new method of reviving wilted plants. As a metrist he has departed widely from his professed original. In this respect he has done wisely, for Pope's measure is quite too uniform for the abrupt changes and varying inflections of a narrative. But too often he weakens a verse by a repetition of trivial monosyllables; as,

> "Wept tears that seemed *to* sweet founts *to* belong."
> "Thou com'st *to* slaughter, *to* depart in joy."

Or by a word not strongly or decidedly enough accented; as,

> "Not *even* yet the alien blood confessed."
> "Lists the soft lapse of the glad waterfall."

We object, also, to his mode of using the Alexandrine as too abrupt. The metre should flow into it with a more gradual and easy swell. One of our own countrymen, Dr. Holmes, has a much surer mastery over this trying measure. We think the subject of metre one to be studied deeply by all who undertake to write in verse. We cannot quite agree with old Samuel Daniel, who, in his noble "Defense of Rime," asserts that "whatsoever form of words doth move, delight, and sway the affections of men, in what Scythian sort soever it be disposed or uttered, that is true number, measure, eloquence, and the perfection of speech." No doubt, the effect produced is the chief point; but in truth, the best utterances of the best minds have never been Scythian, coming to us rather "with their garlands and singing-robes about them."

In conclusion, we should say that vivacity,

rather than strength, was the characteristic of our author; that rapidity of action, rather than depth or originality, was the leading trait of his mind. In his contempt of Laura-Matildaism, he sometimes carries his notions of manliness to an extreme which would be more offensive, were it not altogether absurd. He says, for example, that

> "Even in a love-song man should write for men!"

Imagine the author of the New Timon serenading Lord Stanley, who seems to be an object of his admiration, with "Sleep, gentleman, sleep!" It follows, as a matter of course, that his female characters (the simplest test of a creative poetic genius) are mere shadows.

If we might hazard a guess, we should name Bulwer as the probable author of this poem. It seems hardly possible that it should be the first production of a young writer. The skilfulness with which the plot is constructed, perfection in which is perhaps the slowest attainment of writers of fiction, seems to argue against such a supposition. Moreover, the characters and general sentiment are very much in Bulwer's manner. The fondness for personifying qualities or passions, and of giving a factitious importance to ordinary conceptions by means of initial capitals, is also one of his strongest peculiarities. The moral of the story, too, is within his range. Had we time, we might confirm our theory by a tolerably strong array of minor corroborations. But we must perforce content ourselves with merely throwing out the suggestion. It can hardly be supposed that the authorship of a poem which ran at once through several editions can long remain a secret. The fate of Junius is a warning to all authors not to preserve the anonymous too strictly.

BROWNING'S PLAYS AND POEMS

BROWNING'S PLAYS AND POEMS[1]

"HERE we found an old man in a cavern, so extremely aged as it was wonderful, which could neither see nor go because he was so lame and crooked. The Father, Friar Raimund, said it were good (seeing he was so aged) to make him a Christian; so we christened him." The recollection of this pious action doubtless smoothed the pillow of the worthy Captain Francesco de Ulloa under his dying head; and we mention it here, not because of the credit it confers on the memory of that enterprising and Catholic voyager, but because it reminds us of the manner in which the world treats its poets. Each generation makes a kind of death-bed reparation toward them, and remembers them, so to speak, in its will. It wreathes its superfluous laurel commonly round the trembling temples of age, or lays it ceremoniously on the coffin of him who has passed quite beyond the sphere of its verdict. It deifies those whom it can find no better use for, as a parcel of savages agree that some fragment of wreck, too crooked to be wrought into war-clubs, will make a nice ugly god to worship.

[1] *Paracelsus,* a Poem. By ROBERT BROWNING. London: Effingham Wilson. 1835.

Sordello, a Poem. By ROBERT BROWNING. London: Edward Moxon. 1840.

Bells and Pomegranates. By ROBERT BROWNING. London: Edward Moxon. 1841-46.

Formerly, a man who wished to withdraw himself from the notice of the world retired into a convent. The simpler modern method is, to publish a volume of poems. The surest way of making one's self thoroughly forgotten and neglected is to strive to leave the world better than we find it. Respectable ghosts find it necessary to cut Shelley till the ban of atheism be taken off, though his son is a baronet,—a circumstance, one would think, which ought to have some weight in the land of shadows. Even the religious Byron is forced to be a little shy of him. Mr. Gifford, the *ci-devant* shoemaker, still sends a shudder through the better classes in Elysium, by whispering that Keats was a stable-boy and the friend of Hunt. Milton, to be sure, was seen shaking hands with him on his arrival; but everybody knows what *he* was. Burns sings rather questionable songs in a corner, with a parcel of Scotchmen who smell of brimstone. Coleridge preaches, with Lamb for a congregation.

Ever the same old story. The poor poet is put off with a draft upon Posterity, but it is made payable to the order of Death, and must be indorsed by him to be negotiable. And, after all, who is this respectable fictitious paymaster? Posterity is, to the full, as great a fool as we are. His ears differ not from ours in length by so much as a hair's breadth. He, as well as we, sifts carefully in order to preserve the chaff and bran. He is as much given to paying his debts in shinplasters as we. But, even were Posterity an altogether solvent and trustworthy personage, it would be no less a piece of cowardice and dishonesty in us to shift our proper responsibilities upon his shoulders. If he pay any debts of ours, it is because he defrauds his own contemporary creditors. We have no right thus to speculate prospectively, and to indulge ourselves in a posthumous insolvency. In point of fact, Posterity is no better than a Mrs. Harris. Why, we ourselves have once enjoyed this antenatal grandeur. We were Posterity to that Sarah Gamp, the last generation. We laugh in our sleeves, as we think of it. That we should have been appealed to by so many patriots, philosophers, poets, projectors, and what not, as a convenient embodiment of the eternal justice, and yet be nothing more than the Smiths and Browns over again, with all our little *cliques,* and prejudices, and stupid admirations of ourselves!

We do not, therefore, feel especially flattered, when it is said, that America is a posterity to the living English author. Let us rather wish to deserve the name of a contemporary public unbiased by personal and local considerations. In this way, our geographical position may tend to produce among us a class of competent critics, who, by practice in looking at foreign works from a point of pure art, may in time be able to deal exact justice to native productions.

Unfortunately, before we can have good criticism, it is necessary that we should have good critics; and this consummation seems only the farther off now that the business has grown into a profession and means of subsistence. Doubtless, the critic sets out with an ideal before him. His forereaching spirit shapes to itself designs of noble and gigantic proportions. Very early in life, he even conceives of reading the books he reviews. Soon, however, like other mortals, he comes to consider that merely to get along is a current substitute for success. He finds that in this, as in other professions, the adroitness lies in making the least information go the greatest way. The system is, perhaps, to be blamed rather than we unfortunates who are the victims of it. Poor Zoilus must have his chronic illuminations. He must be statistical, brilliant, profound, withering, scorching, searching, and slashing, once a quarter, or once a month, according to the demands of that insatiable demon of the press to whom he has sold himself. The public have paid for their seats, and, when the curtain rises, he must fulfil the promise of the bills. He must dance, if it be to no better orchestra than Saint Vitus's fiddle. There is no such thing as returning the money at the door. If Zoilus encounter a book which happens to be beyond his comprehension,—are we going too far, or shall we make a clean breast, and acknowledge that this is no unheard-of contingency?—and find it impossible to say what is in it, he must get over the difficulty by telling all his readers what is *out* of it, and by assuring them, with a compassionate regret, that they will not find this or that there. Whether they ought to be there or not is entirely out of the question. The intention of a book is just the last thing to be considered. It were a kind of impiety to suspect any marks of design in it.

The critic is debarred by his position from that common sanctuary of humanity, the confession of ignorance. Were Hamlet to be published anonymously to-morrow, he must tell the public their opinion of it. He may fly for refuge to the Unities. Or he may study the ancient oracles, and ensconce himself in a windier than Delphic ambiguity. Or he may confess to having only *run over* its pages,—a happy phrase, since there is scarce any truly living book which does not bear the print of that hoof which Pindar would have Olympicized into the spurner of dying lions. Moreover, it is considered necessary that every critical journal should have a character,—namely, for one-sidedness, though there is scarce a review that has existed for a dozen years which might not lay claim to as many sides as Goethe, if it were allowed to reckon the number of times it had shifted them. All reviews may be distinguished as Conservative or Liberal, and may be classed together as Illiberal. Ornithologically they might be described as,—ORDO, *Accipitres;* GENUS, *Strix;* SUBGENUS, *Illiberal;* SPECIES, *Conservative* or *Liberal;* food, chiefly authors. One class is under contract to admire every author entirely without brains,—the other, to perform the same ceremony for him who has just enough to allow of a crack in them. They perform alternately the functions of Lucina and Charon. Sometimes it oddly enough chances that they undertake their duties simultaneously, and one is ushering an author into the world with prophecies of long life and prosperity, while the other is as gravely ferrying him out of it. If one stand godfather to a book, the other forthwith enters as coroner with a verdict of "found dead." Not unfrequently each unites in himself the two characters, and assists at the christening of some poor lump that never had life in it at all. In this way, every author has the inestimable privilege accorded him of sitting on two stools. If he have much of a soul in him, he kicks them both over; if not, he subsides quietly between them and disappears forever.

The necessary consequence of this state of things is, that no book is measured by any standard of art. It is commended precisely in proportion as it has vibrated more or less widely on this or that side of the calm centre of rest into the misty region of partisanship. Or, yet worse, it is not the book, but the author, that is reviewed. This simplifies the matter still more. We borrow a man's book merely to knock him over the sconce with, and in nine cases out of ten it is heavy enough to do the business effectually. It were a great blessing, could the present system be exactly reversed. The critic should write under his own name, while the book to be reviewed should be given him with that of the author carefully erased from the title-page. This lion's hide of anonymousness, what does it not cover! Wrapped in that, how safely does the small critic literally bray some helpless giant to death in his critical mortar! It would be well for all of us, if we could be more thoughtful of our responsibilities, if we could remember that for us also that inexorable *janua Ditis,* the pastry-cook's shop, stands always open, that in the midst of literary life we are in the hands of the trunk-maker.

The mistake which lies at the bottom of all this confusion has been the supposition, that there is no absolute standard of excellence to which a book may be referred. It has been taken for granted, that the critic, as well as the poet, is born. And, indeed, though man is said to be the only animal which comes into the world entirely helpless, it would seem that an exception might be made in favor of the critic. He is often fully as competent to his task on the day of his birth, as at any other period during his life; we might even say fitter. For, let him but make any dithyrambic pen-scratches upon a piece of paper, and the Society of Northern Antiquaries would discover therein a copy of some Runic inscription; whereas even that enthusiastic body of scholars might fail to detect any latent meaning in the seemingly clearer productions of his maturer years. If the writing of books belong to one sphere of art, the writing of reviews belongs to another and more ingenious one. The two accomplishments make a happy antithesis. If the author endeavor to show how much he knows, the critic, on the contrary, seems striving to prove how much he can be ignorant of. The comprehension of our own ignorance is the latest and most difficult acquisition of experience. Is the critic to be blamed, that he starts in life without it? There are some things which he understands, and some which he does not. The defect of his mind is, that he cannot distinguish with enough precision between these two classes of ideas.

We wish it to be distinctly understood, that we are speaking of criticism upon works of art alone. With mere rhymers the critic ought to have nothing to do. Time will satirize and silence them effectually enough. For it is only in regard to judgment upon works of art that inspiration is conceded to the critic. For this only, no natural aptness, no previous study, is deemed necessary. Here reigns an unmixed democracy. One man's want of taste is just as good as another's, and it is the inalienable birthright of both. To pass sentence on a President's Message, or a Secretary's Report, one needs to be up with the front of the time in his statistics and his political history. A half-hour's reading in Johnson's "Lives of the Poets" will furnish him with phrases enough to lay Wordsworth on the shelf forever.

We have not alluded yet to the greatest stumbling-block in the way of the critic. His position is not so much that of a teacher as of a representative. He is not expected to instruct, but rather to reflect, his constituency. He may be prejudiced or ignorant himself, as it happens, but he must be the exponent of their united ignorance and prejudice. What they expect to be furnished with is their own opinion, not his. For, in a matter of æsthetics, it is pretty generally conceded, that instinct is a greater matter than any amount of cultivation. Then, too, the larger proportion of the critic's constituents are a mob who consider their education as completed, and there is no ignorance so impenetrable or so dangerous as a half-learning satisfied with itself. For education, as we commonly practise it, amounts simply to the rooting out of God's predilections and the planting of our own in their stead. Every indigenous germ is carefully weeded away, and the soil exhausted in producing a scanty alien crop. The safe instincts of nature are displaced by conventional sciolisms.

Accordingly, whenever Phœbus summons a new ministry, the critic finds himself necessarily in opposition. The only intrinsic evidence which anything can bring with it, that it is fresh from the great creative heart of nature, is its entire newness. Nature never made anything old. Yet are wrinkles the only stamp of genuineness which the critic feels safe in depending upon. He is delighted if he find something like Pope or Goldsmith, and triumphantly takes to task the unfortunate poet who is unclassical enough to be simply like himself. Original minds are never wedge-shaped. They thrust themselves with a crushing bluntness against the prejudices of a dogmatic public. Only the humorist can steal a march upon the world. His weapon has the edge of Mimer's sword, and many an ancient fallacy finds the head loose upon its shoulders in attempting to shake a smiling denial of the decollation.

It has been a fortunate circumstance for German literature, that those who first gave a tone to the criticism of poetry were themselves poets. They best could interpret the laws of art who were themselves concerned in the making of them. In England, on the other hand, those who should have been simple codifiers usurped a legislative function, and poetry has hardly yet recovered from the injury done it by such men as Gifford and Jeffrey. Poetry was measured by a conventional, not an absolute, standard,—the ocean sounded with a ten-foot pole! Uniformity supplanted unity, polish was allowed to pass muster for strength, and smoothness was an adequate substitute for depth. Nothing was esteemed very good, save what was a repetition of something originally not the best. The one drop of original meaning must go through endless homœopathic dilutions. That only was poetry which the critics could have written themselves. A genius was one whose habits shocked the prejudices of his less gifted fellow-citizens, and whose writings never did,—who was unlike everybody else in his life, and exactly like everybody else in his works. The annotation of some incautious commentator has dethroned the soul of Sir John Cheke from its mysterious excarnation in Milton's sonnet. But there is a sound in the name suggestive of such gentlest commonplace, that we can almost fancy its office to have been to transmigrate through many generations of these geniuses. We even think we could point out the exact locality of its present dwelling-place.

The system which erected ordinary minds into the judges and arbiters of extraordinary ones is quite too flattering to be easily overthrown. The deduction of a set of rules, and those founded wholly in externals, from the writings of the poets of any particular age, for the government of all their successors, was a scheme worthy of Chinese exactitude in sameness. Unfortunately, too, the rules, such as they are, were made up from very narrow and limited originals. A smooth fidelity to the artificial, and not truth to nature, was established as the test of true poetry. So strict was the application, that even Doctor Darwin, who, but for this, might have been as great a poet as Hayley, was found guilty of an occasional extravagance. That the criticisms on poetry which were written in the English tongue thirty or forty years ago were serious would seem incredible, could we not confute our doubts by reference to living specimens. Criticism is no more in earnest now than then. One phase of half-learning has only taken the place of another. It still busies itself about words and phrases, syllables, feet, and accents, still forgets that it is the soul only which is and keeps alive. Now, though we have been compelled to enlarge the circle of our poetical sympathies, whether we would or not, and to admit as even great poets writers who were originally received with a universal hoot of critical derision, the same narrow principle governs us still. We continue to condemn one poet by the merits of another, instead of commending him for his own, and, after vainly resisting the claims of Wordsworth and Coleridge, we endeavor to quash all new ones by a comparison with them. All that we would suggest to our brother critics is, that they should be willing to be delighted, and that they should get rid of the idea that it is a weakness to be pleased. Let us consider if we have not esteemed it necessary to impress upon the poets a certain superiority of nature, lest they might combine to dethrone us. Have we not put ourselves somewhat in the condition of that Spanish commander who, having assured the savages that he was a child of the sun, was thenceforward constrained to express a contempt for whatever gold he saw, though that was the very thing he had come in search of?

In the matter of versification, we have been especially incautious. Here, at least, was a purely mechanical process, where the ground was firm beneath our feet. Hath not a critic ears? Hath he not fingers on which he can number as high as ten, recounting the two thumbs for an Alexandrine? Do we not see in this a complete natural outfit, demanding only the coexistence of a mathematical proficiency to the extent we have hinted? There are critics yet living—we shudder to say it, but remember that Mormonism were incredible, had we not ourselves seen it—who sincerely believe that poets construct their verses by such digital enumeration. We might account on this principle (since it would be absurd to suppose them intentional) for the occasional roughnesses in Shakspeare. Perhaps he lost a finger in one of those poaching expeditions of his, and the bitterness with which he must have felt his loss, after he had taken up his final profession, will furnish the commentators with additional proof that all his stupid justices were intended as gibes at Sir Thomas Lucy. At the same time, the bountiful foresight of Providence in regard to our own ears might lead us to suspect the presence of such useful ornaments in the poet also.

If Sir Thomas Browne had suggested remorse for having attempted to define the limits of poetry as a reason for Aristotle's drowning himself in the Euripus, there had been at least some smack of poetical justice in the suicide. There never has been a great work of art which did not in some particular transcend old rules and establish new ones of its own. Newness, boldness, self-sustained strength, these are the characteristics of such works as the world will sooner or later take to its heart. Yet have we critics deemed it possible to establish a formula, by which, given pen, ink, paper, and subject, a wholly unknown quantity (and quality) of immortality might be obtained. We would confine genius to what we can understand of the processes by which some other and perhaps inferior mind produced its results. We would, in fact, establish the measure of our own intellects as the measure of truth and beauty. For the law of elective affinities governs in the region of soul as well as in chemistry, and we absorb and assimilate just so much of an author as we are naturally capable of, and no effort will enable us to take up a particle more. The rest of him does not exist for us, and yet may have a very definite existence notwithstanding. The critic, who tries everything by his own peculiar idiosyncrasy, looks for and finds nothing but himself in the author he reviews; and the consequence is, that what he considers criticisms are nothing more than unconscious confessions of his own mental deficiencies. Instead of exchanging gifts with the poet, he finds himself in a state of war with him, and so, shutting up his mind like the temple of Janus, cuts off from the god within his view before and after, and limits him to such contemplation of his own walls as the darkness will allow.

We have been speaking of criticisms upon what truly deserve the name of works of art, and we consider art not as a quality innate in the soul of genius, but as a law transcending and governing that. It is in the faculty of obedience that genius is superior. Study and effort produce the adroit artificer, not the artist. Talent is capable of perceiving particular applications of this law, but it is only genius which can comprehend it as a harmonious whole. We do not mean to say that successful artifice does not give pleasure to the mind; but it is pleasure of an inferior kind, whose root analysis would discover no deeper than in the emotion of surprise. Construction includes the whole of talent, but is included in genius. It is commonly the last faculty of genius which becomes conscious and active. For genius apparently becomes first aware of a heavenly energy and power of production, and is for a time satisfied with the activity of simple development. We are struck with this fact in the earlier poems of Shakspeare. We find in them only a profuse life, a robust vivacity of all the senses and faculties, without definite direction. Yet very shortly afterward we hear him

"Desiring this man's art and that man's scope."

Genius feels a necessity of production,—talent, a desire to produce an effect. The stimulus in the one case is from within, and in the other from without.

Are we to suppose that the genius for poetry is entirely exhausted? Or would it not rather be wiser to admit as a possibility that the poems we are criticising may be new and great, and to bestow on them a part at least of that study which we dare not refuse to such as have received the warrant of time? The writings of those poets who are established beyond question as great are constantly inculcating upon us lessons of humility and distrust of self. New depths and intricacies of meaning are forever unfolding themselves. We learn by degrees that we had at first comprehended, as it were, only their astral spirit.

Slowly, and, as it might seem, almost reluctantly, their more ethereal and diviner soul lets itself become visible to us, consents to be our interpreter and companion. The passage which one mood of our mind found dark and shadowy, another beholds winding as between the pillars of the Beautiful Gate. We discover beauties in exact proportion as we have faith that we shall. And the old poets have this advantage, that we bring to the reading of them a religious and trustful spirit. The realm of Shakspeare, peopled with royal and heroic shades, the sublime solitudes of Milton, bid us take the shoes from off our feet. Flippancy is abashed there, and conceit startles at the sound of its own voice; for the making of true poetry is almost equally divided between the poet and the reader. To the consideration of universally acknowledged masterpieces we are willing to contribute our own share, and to give earnest study and honest endeavor. Full of meaning was that ancient belief, that the spirits of wood, and water, and rock, and mountain would grant only an enforced communion. The compulsion they awaited was that of a pure mind and a willing spirit.

The critic, then, should never compress the book he comments on within the impoverishing limits of a mood. He should endeavor rather to estimate an author by what he is than by what he is not. He should test the parts of a poem, not by his own preconceptions, but by the motive and aim of the whole. He should try whether, by any possibility, he can perceive a unity in it toward which the several parts centre. He should remember that very many excellent and enlightened men, in other respects good citizens, have esteemed poetry to be, not only an art, but the highest of all arts, round which the rest of what we call the fine arts revolve, receiving light and warmth. He should consider that only they whose understandings are superior to and include that of the artist can criticise his work by intuition. He should feel that his duty is to follow his author, and not to guide him. Above all, he should consider that the effort which the poor author has made to please the world was very likely not intended as a personal insult to be indignantly resented, but should make an attempt to read the book he is about to pronounce judgment upon, and that, too, with a civil attention.

The difference between a true poet and a mere rhymer is not one of degree, but of kind. It is as great as that between the inventor and the mechanician. The latter can make all the several parts of the machine, and adapt them to each other with a polished nicety. The idea once given, he can always reproduce the complete engine. The product of his labor is the highest finish of which brass and steel are capable, but it remains a dead body of metal still. The inventor alone can furnish these strong, weariless limbs with a soul. In his creative intellect resides the spirit of life which shall inspire this earth-born Titan, which shall set him at work in the forge and the mill, and compel him to toil side by side in friendly concert with the forces of nature. There, in the dark, patiently delves the hundred-handed Pyrophagus, and it is this primal breath of the master's spirit which forever gives motion and intelligence to that iron brain and those nerves of steel.

The first thing that we have to demand of a poet is, that his verses be really alive. Life we look for first, and growth as its necessary consequence and indicator. And it must be an original, not a parasitic life,—a life capable of reproduction. There will be barnacles which glue themselves fast to every intellectual movement of the world, and seem to possess in themselves that power of motion which they truly diminish in that which sustains them and bears them along. But there are also unseen winds which fill the sails, and stars by which the courses are set. The oak, which lies in the good ship's side an inert mass, still lives in the green progeny of its chance-dropped acorns. The same gale which bends the creaking mast of pine sings through the tossing hair of its thousand sons in the far inland. The tree of the mechanic bears only wooden acorns.

Is Robert Browning, then, a poet? Our knowledge of him can date back seven years, and an immortality which has withstood the manifold changes of so long a period can be, as immortalities go, no mushroom. How many wooden gods have we seen during that period transformed into chopping-blocks, or kindled into unwilling and sputtering sacrificial fires upon the altars of other deities as ligneous as themselves!

We got our first knowledge of him from two verses of his which we saw quoted in a newspaper, and from that moment took him for granted as a new poet. Since then we have watched him with a constantly deepening interest. Much that seemed obscure and formless in his earlier productions has been interpreted by his later ones. Taken by itself, it might remain obscure and formless still, but it becomes clear and assumes definite shape when considered as only a part of a yet unfinished whole. We perceive running through and knitting together all his poems the homogeneous spirit, gradually becoming assured of itself, of an original mind. We know not what higher praise to bestow on him than to say that his latest poems are his best.

His earlier poems we shall rather choose to consider as parts and illustrations of his poetic life than as poems. We find here the consciousness of wings, the heaven grasped and measured by the aspiring eye, but no sustained flight as yet. These are the poet's justifications of himself to himself, while he was brooding over greater designs. They are the rounds of the ladder by which he has climbed, and more interesting for the direction they indicate than from any intrinsic worth. We would not be considered as undervaluing them. Had he written nothing else, we should allow them as heights attained, and not as mere indications of upward progress. But Mr. Browning can afford to do without them. And if he has not yet fully expressed himself, if we can as yet see only the lower half of the statue, we can in some measure foretell the whole. We can partly judge whether there is likely to be in it the simplicity and comprehensiveness, the poise, which indicates the true artist. At least, we will not judge it by its base, however the sculptor's fancy may have wreathed it with graceful or grotesque arabesques, to render it the worthy footstool of his crowning work. Above all, let us divert ourselves of the petty influences of contemporaneousness, and look at it as if it were just unburied from the enbalming lava of Pompeii. Is the eye of the critic so constituted, that it can see only when turned backward?

Mr. Browning's first published poem was Paracelsus.[2] This was followed by Strafford, a Tragedy, of which we know only that it was "acted at the Theatre Royal, Covent Garden." We do not need it in order to get a distinct view of his steady poetical growth. Next comes Sordello, a Poem; and the list is completed by Bells and Pomegranates, a series of lyrical and dramatic poems published at intervals during the last six years. Were we to estimate Paracelsus and Sordello separately and externally as individual poems, without taking into consideration their antecedent or consequent internal relations, we should hardly do justice to the author. Viewed by itself, Sordello would incline us to think that Mr. Browning had lost in simplicity, clearness,

[2] This is, of course, incorrect. "Pauline" was published two years earlier than "Paracelsus," in 1833.—Ed.

and directness of aim, in compactness and decision of form, and in unity of effect. We may as well say bluntly, that it is totally incomprehensible as a connected whole. It reminds one of Coleridge's epigram on his own Ancient Mariner:—

"Your poem must eternal be,
Dear Sir, it cannot fail;
For 'tis incomprehensible,
And without head or tail."

It presents itself to us, at first view, as a mere nebulosity, triumphantly defying the eye to concentrate itself on any one point. But if we consider it intently, as possibly having some definite relation to the author's poetic life, we begin to perceive a luminous heart in the midst of the misty whirl, and, indeed, as a natural consequence of it. By dint of patient watchfulness through such telescope as we possess, we have even thought that it might not be wholly incapable of resolution as a system by itself. It is crowded full of images, many of them truly grand. Here and there it opens cloudily, and reveals glimpses of profound thought and conception of character. The sketch of Taurello, the Italian captain of the Middle Ages, drawn rapidly, as with a bit of charcoal on a rough wall, is masterly. Perhaps we should define what is in itself indefinable as well as may be, if we say that we find in Sordello the materials of a drama, profuse, but as yet in formless solution, not crystallized firmly round the thread of any precise plot, but capable of it. We will say that it was a fine poem before the author wrote it. In reading it, we have seemed to ourselves to be rambling along some wooded ridge in the tropics. Here gigantic vines clamber at random, hanging strange trees with clusters that seem dipped in and dripping with the sluggish sunshine. Here we break our way through a matted jungle, where, nevertheless, we stumble over giant cactuses in bloom, lolling delighted in the sultry air. Now and then a gap gives us a glimpse of some ravishing distance, with a purple mountain-peak or two, and all the while clouds float over our heads, gorgeous and lurid, which we may consider as whales or camels, just as our Polonian fancy chooses.

A book is often termed obscure and unintelligible by a kind of mental *hypallage,* which exchanges the cases of the critic and the thing criticised. But we honestly believe that Sordello is enveloped in mists, of whose begetting we are quite guiltless. It may have a meaning, but, as the logicians say, *a posse ad esse non valet argumentum.* Or the meaning may be in the same category with those flitting islands of the Canary group, which vanished as soon as seen, and of which stout Sir John Hawkins says mournfully, that "it should seem he was not yet born to whom God hath appointed the finding of them." Obscurity is a luxury in which no young author has a right to indulge himself. We allow writers of established reputations to tax our brains to a limited extent, because we expect to find something, and feel a little natural delicacy about confessing that we come back from the search without a mare's egg or so, at the very least. Then, too, there are some writers whose obscurity seems to be their chief merit. Of these, some of the Persian religious poets, and, above all, the "later Platonists," may serve as examples. These have a title by prescription to every imaginable form of obfuscation. When we hear that anyone has retired into obscurity, we can fancy him plunging into the speculations of these useful men. Before we had seen the *Epistolæ Obscurorum Virorum,* we took it for granted as a collection of their correspondence, though we found it hard to conceive of any contemporary class of persons who corresponded with them in the smallest particular.

We do not by any means join in the vulgar demand, that authors should write down to the average understanding; because we have faith that this understanding is becoming equal to higher and higher tasks from year to year. Nor should we be thankful for that simplicity which many inculcate, and by which they mean that an author should be as artificial and as flat as he can. The simplicity of one age can never be that of the next. That which was natural to Homer would be a mechanical contrivance now. Our age is eminently introspective. It is constantly asking itself (with no very satisfactory result), Whence? and Whither? and though seven cities quarreled over one limb of this problem after Homer's death, it is hardly probable that he ever asked himself the question, whence he came, or whither he was going, in the whole course of his life. Our poets do not sing to an audience who can neither read nor write. The persons who pay for their verses are not a half-dozen of petty kings, who would not (as the boys say) know B from a bull's foot, and the polish of whose courts would be pretty well paralleled in that of his present Gracious Majesty of Ashantee. The law of demand and supply rules everywhere, and we doubt not that Apollo composed bucolics in words of one syllable for the edification of his serene dunceship Admetus. His sheep (a less critical audience) may have heard grander music, of which Orpheus perhaps caught echoes among the hills. We cannot have back the simplicity of the age to which it was addressed. Our friend Jinks, who is so clamorous for it, must wear raw bull's-hide, or that still less expensive undress of Sir Richard Blackmore's Pict. The reading public cannot have its cake and eat it too, still less can it have the cake which it ate two thousand years ago. Moreover, we are not Greeks, but Goths; and the original blood is still so vivacious in our veins, that our rustic architects, though admitting, as a matter of pure æsthetics, that all modern meeting-houses should be exact Grecian temples or tombs (steeple and all), will yet contrive to smuggle a pointed window somewhere into the back of the building, or the belfry.

Having glanced confusedly at Sordello, as far as it concerns ourselves, let us try if we can discover that it has any more distinct relation to the author. And here we ought naturally to take it in connection with Paracelsus. From this point of view, a natural perspective seems to arrange itself, and a harmony is established between the two otherwise discordant poems. Paracelsus, then, appears to us to represent, and to be the outlet of, that early life of the poet which is satisfied with aspiration simply; Sordello, that immediately succeeding period when power has become conscious, but exerts itself for the mere pleasure it feels in the free play of its muscles, without any settled purpose. Presently we shall see that it has defined and concentrated itself, and set about the production of solid results. There is not less power; it is only deeper, and does not dissipate itself over so large a surface. The range is not narrower, but choicer.

Let us now turn to the Bells and Pomegranates. And here we are met on the very threshold by the difficulty of selection. Not only are the lyrics singularly various in tone and character, but, in the dramas, that interdependence of the parts, which is one of their most striking and singular merits, makes any passage taken by itself do great injustice to the author. These dramas are not made up of a number of beauties, distinct and isolate as pearls, threaded upon the string of the plot. Each has a permeating life and spirit of its own. When we would break off any fragments, we cannot find one which would by itself approach completeness. It is like tearing away a limb from a living body. For these are works of art in the truest sense. They are not aggregations of dissonant beauties, like some modern sculptures, against which the Apollo might bring an action of trover for an arm, and the Antinoüs for a leg, but pure statues, in which everything superfluous has been sternly chiselled away, and whose wonderful balance might seem tameness to the ordinary observer, who demands *strain* as an evidence of strength. They are not arguments on either side of any of the great questions which divide the world. The characters in them are not bundles of different characteristics, but their gradual development runs through the whole drama and makes the life of it. We do not learn what they are by what they say of themselves, or by what is said of them, so much as by what they do or leave undone. Nor does any drama seem to be written for the display of some one character which the author has conceived and makes a favorite of. No undue emphasis is laid upon any. Each fills his part, and each, in his higher or lower grade, his greater or less prominence, is equally necessary to the rest. Above all, his personages are not mere mouthpieces for the author's idiosyncrasies. We take leave of Mr. Browning at the end of Sordello, and, except in some shorter lyrics, see no more of him. His men and women *are* men and women, and not Mr. Browning masquerading in different-colored dominos. We implied as much when we said that he was an artist. For the artist-period begins precisely at the point where the pleasure of expressing self ends, and the poet becomes sensible that his highest duty is to give voice to the myriad forms of nature, which, wanting him, were dumb. The term *art* includes many lower faculties of the poet; but this appears to us its highest and most comprehensive definition. Hence Shakspeare, the truest of artists, is also nothing more than a voice. We seek in vain in his plays for any traces of his personal character or history. A man may be even a great poet without being an artist. Byron was, through all whose works we find no individual, self-subsistent characters. His heroes are always himself in so many different stage-costumes, and his Don Juan is his best poem, and approaches more nearly a work of art, by just so much as he has in that expressed himself most truly and untheatrically.

Regarding Mr. Browning's dramas in this light, and esteeming them as so excellent and peculiar, we shall not do him the injustice of picking out detached beauties, and holding them up as fair specimens of his power. For his wholeness is one great proof of this power. He may be surpassed by one contemporary in finish, by another in melody; but we shall not try him by comparison. We are thankful to him for being what he is, for contriving to be himself and to keep so. Why, in ordinary society, is it not sometimes the solitary merit of Smith, and all that makes him endurable, that he is not exactly Brown? We are quite willing to be grateful for whatever gifts it has pleased God to bestow on any musically-endowed spirit. The scale is composed of various notes, and cannot afford to do without any of them, or to have one substituted for another.

It is not so much for his expression of isolated thoughts as for his power of thinking, that we value Browning. Most readers prefer those authors in whom they find the faculty of observation, to those in whom power of thought is predominant, for the simple reason, that sensation is easier than reflection. By observation we mean that quality of mind which discriminates and sets forth particular ideas by and for themselves alone. Thought goes deeper, and employs itself in detecting and exemplifying the unity which embraces and underlies all ideas. A writer of the first class reaches the mass of readers because they can verify what he says by their own experience, and we cannot help thinking tolerably well of those who put us in mind of our own penetration. He requires them only to feel. A writer of the other kind taxes the understanding, and demands in turn an exercise of thought on the part of his readers. Both of these faculties may, of course, differ in degree, may be more or less external, more or less profound, as it may happen. They coexist in the same mind, overlapping one the other by a wider or more limited extent. The predominance of one or the other determines the tendency of the mind. Those are exceptional natures in which they balance each other as in Shakspeare. We may instance Browne and

Montaigne as examples in one kind, Bacon as an illustration of the other.

It is because we find in Browning eminent qualities as a dramatist, that we assign him his place as a thinker. This dramatic faculty is a far rarer one than we are apt to imagine. It does not consist in a familiarity with stage effect, in the capacity for inventing and developing a harmonious and intricate plot, nor in an appreciation of passion as it reveals itself in outward word or action. It lies not in a knowledge of character, so much as in an imaginative conception of the springs of it. Neither each of these singly, nor all of them together, without that unitary faculty which fuses the whole and subjects them all to the motion of a single will, constitute a dramatist. Among the crowd of play-writers contemporary with Shakspeare, we can find poets enough, but can we name three who were dramatists in any other than a technical sense? In endeavoring to eliminate the pure dramatic faculty, by precipitating and removing one by one the grosser materials which it holds in solution, we have left the Greek drama entirely out of the question. The *motive* of the ancient tragedy differs from that of the modern in kind. Nor do we speak of this faculty as a higher or lower one, but simply as being distinct and rare.

Mr. Browning's humor is as genuine as that of Carlyle, and if his laugh have not the "earthquake" character with which Emerson has so happily labeled the shaggy merriment of that Jean Paul Burns, yet it is always sincere and hearty, and there is a tone of meaning in it which always sets us thinking. Had we room, we should be glad to give a full analysis of his Soul's Tragedy, which abounds in the truest humor, flitting from point to point with all the electric sparkle and condensed energy of wit. Wit employs itself about externals and conventionalities. Its merit lies quite as much in nicety of expression as in the idea expressed, or even more. For it is something which may be composed, and is therefore necessarily choice of form. Humor goes deeper, bases itself upon the eternal, and not the ephemeral, relations of things, and is something interfused through the whole nature of the man, and which, forcing him to feel keenly what is hollow in the outward forms of society, often makes him careless of all form. In literature, therefore, we see it overleaping or breaking down all barriers. Wit makes other men laugh, and that only once. It may be repeated indefinitely to new audiences, and produce the same result. Humor makes the humorist himself laugh. He is a part of his humor, and it can never be repeated without loss. If we take the common metaphor, that humor is broader than wit, we shall express well enough its greater carelessness of form and precise limit. It especially behooves a poet, then, to be on his guard against the impulses of his humor. Poetry and humor are subject to different laws of art, and it is dangerous to let one encroach upon the province of the other. It may be questioned, whether verse, which is by nature subject to strict law, be the proper vehicle for humor at all. The contrast, to be sure, between the preciseness of the metrical rule and the frolicsome license of the thought, has something humorous in itself. The greater *swing* which is allowed to the humorous poet in rhythm and rhyme, as well as in thought, may be of service to him, and save him from formality in his serious verses. Undoubtedly the success of Hood's Bridge of Sighs was due in some degree to the quaintness and point of the measure and the rhyme, the secret of which he had learned in his practice as a humorous versifier. But there is danger that the poet, in allowing full scope to this erratic part of his nature, may be brought in time to value form generally at less than its true worth as an element of art. We have sometimes felt a jar in reading Mr. Browning's lyrical poems, when, just as he has filled us full of quiet delight by some touch of pathos or marble gleam of classical beauty, this exuberant geniality suggests some cognate image of the ludicrous, and turns round to laugh in our faces. This necessity of deferring to form in some shape or other is a natural, and not an ingrafted, quality of human nature. It often, laughably enough, leads men, who have been totally regardless of all higher laws, to cling most pertinaciously and conscientiously to certain purely ceremonial observances. If the English courts should ever dispense with so much of their dignity and decorum as consists in horsehair, we have no doubt that the first rogue who shall be sentenced by a wigless judge will be obstinately convinced of a certain unconstitutionality in the proceeding, and feel himself an injured man, defrauded of the full dignity of the justice enjoyed by his ancestors.

There are two faults of which we are chiefly conscious in Mr. Browning's lyrics. The first is a tendency to parenthesize one thought or metaphor within another, and seems to arise from fertility of mind and exuberance of illustration, united with the power of too facile execution. The other is involved in that humorous element of his character which we have noticed, and which gives him so keen an enjoyment of his own thoughts as disqualifies him for distinguishing those of them which will strike all other minds with equal distinctness and force, and those which will be appreciated only by persons constituted like himself. From both these defects his dramas are almost wholly free.

And now, if we could be sure that our readers would read Mr. Browning's poems with the respect and attentive study they deserve, what should hinder us from saying that we think him a great poet? However, as the world feels uncomfortably somewhere, it can hardly tell how or why, at hearing people called great, before it can claim a share in their greatness by erecting to them a monument with a monk-Latin inscription on it which nine-tenths of their countrymen cannot construe, and as Mr. Browning must be as yet comparatively a young man, we will content ourselves with saying that he has in him the elements of greatness. To us he appears to have a wider range and greater freedom of movement than any other of the younger English poets. In his dramas we find always a leading design and a conscientious subordination of all the parts to it. In each one of them also, below the more apparent and exterior sources of interest, we find an illustration of some general idea which bears only a philosophical relation to the particular characters, thoughts, and incidents, and without which the drama is still complete in itself, but which yet binds together and sustains the whole, and conduces to that unity for which we esteem these works so highly. In another respect Mr. Browning's dramatic power is rare. The characters of his women are finely discriminated. No two are alike, and yet the characteristic features of each are touched with the most delicate precision. By far the greater number of authors who have attempted female characters have given us mere automata. They think it enough, if they make them subordinate to a generalized idea of human nature. Mr. Browning never forgets that women *are* women, and not simply human beings, for there they occupy common ground with men.

Many English dramas have been written within a few years, the authors of which have established their claim to the title of poet. We cannot but allow that we find in them fine thoughts finely expressed, passages of dignified and sustained eloquence, and as adequate a conception of character as the reading of history and the study of models will furnish. But it is only in Mr. Browning that we find enough of freshness, vigor, grasp, and of that clear insight and conception which enable the artist to construct characters from within, and so to make them real things, and not images, as to warrant our granting the honor due to the Dramatist.

THE WORKS OF WALTER SAVAGE LANDOR

THE WORKS OF WALTER SAVAGE LANDOR[1]

THOUGH we have placed at the head of our article the title of the collected edition of Landor's works, it is to a consideration of his poems, and in particular of his "Hellenics," that we shall in a great measure devote ourselves. It may at first sight seem somewhat of an anomaly to try a great prose-writer by what he has written in verse; but the man is so individual that the merits both of his prose and poetry are identical in kind, and the defects which we are conscious of in the latter may help us to a clearer understanding, if not to a clearer definition, of what is poetry.

To say of any writer that his faults are peculiarly his own, is in a certain sense to commend him, and, where these are largely outweighed by excellences, it amounts to a verdict in favor of his originality. Imitative minds invariably seize upon and exaggerate the exaggerations of their model. The parasitic plant indicates the cracks, roughnesses, and flaws of the wall to which it clings, for in these alone is it able to root itself. If Byron were morose, a thousand poetasters bleated savagely from under wer-wolves' skins. If Carlyle be Teutonic, those will be found who

[1] *The Works of Walter Savage Landor.* London: Edward Moxon. 1846. 2 v.

will out-Germanize him. If Emerson be mystic, the Emersonidæ can be misty. It is only where the superior mind begins to differ from the commonplace type, or to diverge from the simple orbit of nature, that inferior ones become subject to its attraction. Then they begin to gravitate toward it, are carried along with it, and, when it pauses, are thrown beyond it. It is only the eclipse men stare at. It is not the star but the comet that gathers a tail. When we say, then, that Landor's faults are especially Landor, we imply that he is no imitator. When we say that he has no imitators, we imply that his faults are few.

If we were asked to name a writer to whose style the phrase *correct* would most exactly apply, we should select Landor. Yet it is not so at the expense of warmth, or force, or generosity. It is only bounded on every side by dignity. In all those portions of his works which present him to us most nobly, and therefore most truly, the most noticeable quality of the mere style is its *un*-noticeability. Balance and repose are its two leading characteristics. He has discovered that to be simple is to be classical. He observes measure and proportion in everything. If he throw mud it is by drachm and scruple. His coarsest denunciation may be conveyed in sentences of just so many words spelt in just such a manner. He builds a paragraph as perfect as a Greek temple, no matter whether Phœbus or Anubis is to be housed in it;—for he is a coarse man with the most refined perceptions. He is the

Avatar of John Bull. He is Tom Cribb with the soul of Plato in him, and when he attacks there is no epithet which seems to fit him so well as *bruiser.*

But though he asks us to many banquets, where, after the English fashion, the conversation at a certain point becomes such as to compel women to withdraw; though he so obtrudes his coarseness upon us that any notice of him would be inadequate without some mention of it; yet this jarring element is rather the rare exception than the rule in his writings. It affects the style more than the character of his works, and is more important in helping us to an estimate of the man, than of his books. An introduction to him without a previous hint of it would hardly be fair; yet we might be in his company for hours without discovering it. We should be at a loss to name the writer of English prose who is his superior, or, setting Shakspeare aside, the writer of English who has furnished us with so many or so delicate aphorisms of human nature.

Browning, certainly a competent authority, in dedicating a drama to him, calls him a great dramatic poet, and if we deduct from the dramatic faculty that part of it which has reference to a material stage, we can readily concede him the title. His mind has not the succinctness necessary to a writer for the theatre. It has too decided a tendency to elaboration, and is more competent to present to the mind a particular quality of character in every light of which it is susceptible, than to construct a unitary character out of a combination of qualities. Perhaps we should be more strictly accurate if we should say that his power lies in showing how certain situations, passions, or qualities would affect the thought and speech rather than the action of a character. Of all his dramas except one, he has himself said that they are more imaginary conversations than dramas. Of his "Imaginary Conversations" we may generally say that they would be better defined as dialogues between the imaginations of the persons introduced, than between the persons themselves. There is a something in all men and women who deserve the much-abused title of *individuals,* which we call their *character,* something finer than the man or woman, and yet which *is* the man or woman nevertheless. We feel it in whatever they say or do, but it is better than their speech or deed, and can be conceived of apart from these. It is his own conceptions of the characters of different personages that Landor brings in as interlocutors. Between Shakspeare's historical and ideal personages we perceive no difference in point of reality. They are alike historical to us. We allow him to substitute his Richard for the Richard of history, and we suspect that those are few who doubt whether Caliban ever existed. Whatever Hamlet or Cæsar say we feel to be theirs, though we know it to be Shakspeare's. Whatever Landor puts into the mouth of Pericles and Michel Angelo and Tell, we know to be his, though we can conceive that it might have been theirs. Don Quixote would never have attacked any puppets of his. The hand which jerked the wires and the mouth which uttered the speeches would have been too clearly visible.

We cannot so properly call Landor a great thinker, as a man who has great thoughts. His mind has not much continuity, as, indeed, we might infer from what he himself somewhere says—that his memory is a poor one. He is strong in details and concentrates himself upon points. Hence his criticisms on authors, though always valuable as far as they go, are commonly fragmentary. He makes profound remarks upon certain passages of a poem, but does not seem to aim at a comprehension of the entire poet. He perceives rather than conceives. He is fond of verbal criticism, and takes up an author often in the spirit of a proofreader. He has a microscopic eye, and sees with wonderful distinctness what is immediately before him. When he turns it on a poet it sometimes gives us the same sort of feeling as when Gulliver reports his discoveries in regard to the complexions of the Brobdingnag maids of honor. Yet, of course, it gives him equal power for perceiving every minutest shade of beauty.

In the historical persons whom his conversations introduce to us, or, to speak more strictly, who introduce his conversations to us, we are sensible of two kinds of truth. They are true to the external circumstances and to the history of the times in which they lived, and they are true to Landor. We always feel that it is he who is speaking, and that he has merely chosen a character whom he considered suitable to express a particular phase of his own mind. He never, for a moment, loses himself in his characters. He is never raised or depressed by them, but raises and depresses them at will. If he choose, he will make Pericles talk of Blackwood's Magazine, or Aspasia comment on the last number of the Quarterly Review. Yet all the while every slightest propriety of the household economy and the external life of the Greeks will be observed with rigid accuracy. The anachronism does not seem to be that Pericles and Anaxagoras should discuss the state of England, but that Walter Savage Landor should be talking modern politics in ancient Greek,—so thoroughly are the man's works impregnated with himself. But to understand this fully we must read all his writings. We only mention it as affecting the historical veracity of his characters, and not because it subtracts anything from the peculiar merits which belong to him as a writer. If a character be in *rapport* with his own, he throws into it the whole energy of his powerful magnetism. He translates everything into Landor, just as Chapman is said to have favored Ajax, in his version of the Iliad. After we are once put upon our guard, we find a particular enjoyment in this intense individuality. We understand that he is only borrowing the pulpits of other people to preach his own notions from, and we feel the refreshment which every one experiences in being brought within the more immediate sphere of an original temperament and a robust organization. We discover, at last, that we have encountered an author who from behind a variety of masks can be as personally communicative as Montaigne.

The epithet *robust* seems to us particularly applicable to Landor. And his is the robustness of a naturally vigorous constitution, maintained in a healthy equipoise by regular exercise. The open air breathes through his writings, and in reading him we often have a feeling (to use a local phrase) of *all outdoors*. In saying this we refer to the general freedom of spirit, to the natural independence confirmed by a life of immediate contact with outward nature, and only thrown back the more absolutely on its own resources by occasional and reserved commerce with mankind; tolerated rather than sought by a haughty, and at the same time exquisitely sensitive, disposition. We should add, that his temperament is one more keenly alive to his own interior emotions than those suggested to him from without. Consequently, while a certain purity and refinement suggest an intimacy with woods and fields, the truest and tenderest touches of his pencil are those of human and not of external nature. His mountain scenery is that of the soul; his rural landscapes and his interiors are those of the heart. If there should seem to be a contradiction between the coarseness and the delicacy we have attributed to him, the inconsistency is in himself. We may find the source of both in the solitary habit of his mind. The one is the natural independence of a somewhat rugged organization, whose rough edges have never been smoothed by attrition with the world, and which, unaccustomed to the pliability and mutual accommodation necessary in a crowd, resents every obstacle as intentional, every brush of the elbow as a personal affront. The other has been fostered by that habitual tendency of the isolated to brood over and analyze their own sentiments and emotions. Or shall we say that the rough exterior is assumed as a shield for the tenderness, as certain insects house themselves under a movable roof of lichen? This is sometimes the case, but we suspect that in Landor both qualities are idiosyncratic. That frailest creation of the human imagination, the hamadryad, is the tenant and spirit of the gnarled oak, which grasps the storm in its arms. To borrow a comparison from the Greeks, to whom Landor so constantly refers us, we must remember that Polyphemus, while he was sharpening the spit for Ulysses, was pining for Galatea, and that his unrequited tenderness sought solace in crushing his rival with half a mountain.

There are two kinds of egoism: one which is constantly measuring itself by others, and one which as constantly measures others by itself. This last we call originality. It secludes a man from external influences, and, leaving him nothing to lean upon but his own judgments and impressions, teaches him their value and enables him to inspire other men with the same estimate of them. In this sense Landor is original. This gives all that he writes a decided charm, and makes the better part of it exceedingly precious. He is constructed altogether on a large scale. His littlenesses are great, his weaknesses decided; and as long as the larger part of men are so careful to give us any thing rather than themselves, let us learn to be duly thankful for even a littleness that is sincere, and a weakness that is genuine. So entirely has he been himself, that, while we cannot help being conscious of his deficiencies, we also feel compelled to grant a certain kind of completeness in him. Whatever else he might have been, we are sure that he could not have been more of a Landor. In spite of the seeming contradictions of his character, it would not be easy to find a life and mind more thoroughly consistent than his. A strenuous persistency marks every thing about him. A few friendships and a good many animosities have lasted him all his days. He may add to both, but he never lessens the number of either. In speaking of a man constituted as he is, it would perhaps be better to say oppugnancies than animosities. For an animosity properly implies contemporaneousness, and a personal feeling toward its object; but so entirely does Landor refer every thing to his absolute self, that he will pursue as vindictively a dead error, or a dead man, as a living one. It is as they affect him that they are good or bad. It is not the year 48 or 1848 that is past or present, but simply Walter Savage Landor. With him it is *amicus Plato, amica veritas, magis amicus Landor.* His sense of his own worth is too large and too dignified to admit of personal piques and jealousies. He resents an assault upon himself as a wrong done to sound literature, and accepts commendation merely as a tribute to truth.

We know of no writer whose pages, if opened at random, are more sure to repay us than those of Landor. Nowhere shall we find admirable thoughts more admirably expressed, nowhere sublimer metaphors or more delicate ones, nowhere a mind maintained at a high level more equally, or for longer intervals. There is no author who surpasses, and few who equal him in purity and elevation of style, or in sustained dignity and weight of thought. We should hesitate to name any writings but Shakspeare's which would afford so large and so various a selection of detached passages complete and precious in themselves. The rarest and tenderest emotions of love and friendship have never found a more adequate historian. His pathos is most delicately subdued. He approaches sorrow with so quiet a footfall and so hushing a gesture, that we are fain to suspend our breath and the falling of our tears, lest they should break that tender silence. It is not to look upon a picture of grief, but into the solemn presence of grief herself, that he leads us.

Landor has as little humor as Massinger, who in some respects resembles him, though at an infinite distance below. All that he has is of a somewhat gigantic and clumsy sort. He snatches up some little personage who has offended him, sets him on a high shelf, and makes him chatter and stamp for his diversion. He has so long conversed in imagination with the most illustrious spirits of all ages, that there is a plentiful measure of contempt in his treatment of those he esteems unworthy. His lip begins to curl at sight of a king, partly because he seems to consider men of that employment fools, and partly because he thinks them no gentlemen. For Bourbons he has a particular and vehement contempt, because to the folly of kingship they add the vileness of being Frenchmen. He is a theoretic republican of the strain of Milton, Sydney, and Harrington, and would have all the citizens of his republic far-descended gentlemen and scholars.

It is not wonderful that Landor has never been a popular writer. His is a mind to be quietly appreciated rather than to excite an enthusiastic partisanship. That part of his works which applies immediately to the present is the least valuable. The better and larger portion is so purely imaginative, so truly ideal, that it will be as fresh and true a hundred or a thousand years hence as now. His writings have seldom drawn any notice from the reviews, which is singular only when we consider that he has chosen to converse almost exclusively with the past, and is, therefore, in some sense, a contemporary of those post-secular periodicals. The appearance of a collected edition of his works seems more like the publication of a new edition of Plato than of an author who has lived through the most stirring period of modern history. Not that he does not speak and speak strongly of living men and recent events, but at such times the man is often wholly, or at least partially, obscured in the Englishman.

We should be quite at a loss to give adequate specimens of a man so various. As we stated in the outset, we shall confine ourselves to the "Hellenics," on a brief consideration of which we now enter. They will convince any careful reader that something more (we do not say higher or finer) goes to the making up of a poet than is included in the composition of the most eloquent and forcible of prose-writers.

Opulent as the prose of Landor is, we cannot but be conscious of something like poverty in his verse. He is too minutely circumstantial for a poet, and that tendency of his mind to details, which we before alluded to, stands in his way. The same careful exactness in particulars which gives finish to his prose and represses any tendency to redundance, seems to oppress his verse and to deprive it of flow. He is a poet in his prose, but in his poetry he is almost a proser. His conceptions are in the fullest sense poetical, but he stops just on the hither side of adequate expression. He comes short by so mere a hair's-breadth that there is something painful in it. There is beauty of a certain kind, but the witching grace is wanting.

> "And painfully the soul receives
> Sense of that gone which it had never mist,
> Of somewhat lost, but *when* it never wist."

In verse Landor seems like a person expressing himself in a foreign language. He may attain to perfect accuracy and elegance, but the native ease is out of his reach. We said before that his power lay less in developing a continuous train of thought, than in presenting single thoughts in their entire fullness of portion. But in poetry, it is necessary that each poem should be informed with a homogeneous spirit, which now represses the thought, now forces it to overflow, and everywhere modulates the metre and the cadence by an instinct of which we can understand the operations, though we may be unable to define the mode of them. Beside this, we should say that Landor possessed a *choice* of language, and is not possessed by that irresistible and happy necessity of the true poet toward the particular word whose place no other can be made to fit. His nicety in specialties imprisons him for the time in each particular verse or passage, and the poem seems not to have grown, but to have been built up slowly, with square, single bricks, each carefully molded, pressed, and baked beforehand. Sometimes, where a single thought or feeling is to be expressed, he appears exactly the man for the occasion.

We must not be supposed to deny the presence, in Landor's "Hellenics," of those fine qualities which we admire in his prose. We mean that the beauties are not specially those of poetry, and that they gain nothing from the verse. The almost invisible nerves of the most retired emotions are traced with rapid and familiar accuracy, rare shades of sentiment and character are touched with a delicacy peculiar to Landor, noble thoughts are presented to us, and metaphors fresh from nature. But we find no quality here which is not in his prose. The "Hellenics" seem like admirable translations of original poems. It would be juster, perhaps, to say that they impress us as Greek poetry does. We appreciate the poet more than the poetry, in which the Northern mind feels an indefinable lack.

The "Hellenics" have positive merits, but they are not exclusively those of poetry. They belong to everything which Landor has written. We should mention, as especially prominent, entire clearness, and so thorough an absorption of the author in his subject that he does not cast about him for something to say, but is only careful of what he shall reject. He does not tell us too much, and wound our self-esteem by always taking it for granted that we do not know anything, and can not imagine anything.

We should be inclined to select as favorable specimens of his poetry, *"Thrasymedes and Eunoë," "The Hamadryad," "Enallos and Cymodameia,"* and the last poem of the "Hellenics," to which no title is prefixed. Of these the last is most characteristic of Landor and of his scholarly and gentlemanlike love of freedom; but the one most likely to be generally pleasing is the *"Hamadryad."*

In this brief article we have not attempted

anything like an adequate criticism of one of the most peculiar and delightful writers in the English language. We have only stated some of the sharper impressions of him which remain in our memory, after an acquaintance of many years. We feel that what we have said is exceedingly imperfect. But we shall be satisfied if we lead any one to desire that better knowledge of him which his works alone can furnish. To give an idea of the character of the man, a very few quotations would suffice, but to show the value of his writings we should be obliged to copy nearly all of them. We are sometimes inclined to think of Wordsworth, that, if he has not reduced poetry to the level of commonplace, he has at least glorified commonplace by elevating it into the diviner æther of poetry; and we may say of Landor that he has clothed common-sense with the singing-robes of imagination. In this respect he resembles Goethe, and we feel that he eminently deserves one of the titles of the great German—the Wise, for, as common-sense dwelling in the ordinary plane of life becomes experience and prudence, so, looking down from the summits of imagination, she is heightened into inspiration and wisdom.

PALFREY'S HISTORY OF NEW ENGLAND

PALFREY'S HISTORY OF NEW ENGLAND[1]

THE history of New England is written imperishably on the face of a continent, and in characters as beneficent as they are enduring. In the Old World national pride feeds itself with the record of battles and conquests;—battles which proved nothing and settled nothing; conquests which shifted a boundary on the map, and put one ugly head instead of another on the coin which the people paid to the tax-gatherer. But wherever the New-Englander travels among the sturdy commonwealths which have sprung from the seed of the Mayflower, churches, schools, colleges, tell him where the men of his race have been, or their influence penetrated; and an intelligent freedom is the monument of conquests whose results are not to be measured in square miles. Next to the fugitives whom Moses led out of Egypt, the little ship-load of outcasts who landed at Plymouth two centuries and a half ago are destined to influence the future of the world. The spiritual thirst of mankind has for ages been quenched at Hebrew fountains; but the embodiment in human institutions of truths uttered by the Son of Man eighteen centuries ago was to be mainly the work of Puritan thought and Puri-

[1] *History of New England during the Stuart Dynasty.* By JOHN GORHAM PALFREY. Vol. III. Boston: Little, Brown & Co. 1864.

tan self-devotion. Leave New England out in the cold! While you are plotting it, she sits by every fireside in the land where there is piety, culture, and free thought.

Faith in God, faith in man, faith in work,—this is the short formula in which we may sum up the teaching of the founders of New England, a creed ample enough for this life and the next. If their municipal regulations smack somewhat of Judaism, yet there can be no nobler aim or more practical wisdom than theirs; for it was to make the law of man a living counterpart of the law of God, in their highest conception of it. Were they too earnest in the strife to save their souls alive? That is still the problem which every wise and brave man is life-long in solving. If the Devil take a less hateful shape to us than to our fathers, he is as busy with us as with them; and if we cannot find it in our hearts to break with a gentleman of so much worldly wisdom, who gives such admirable dinners, and whose manners are so perfect, so much the worse for us.

Looked at on the outside, New England history is dry and unpicturesque. There is no rustle of silks, no waving of plumes, no clink of golden spurs. Our sympathies are not awakened by the changeful destinies, the rise and fall, of great families, whose doom was in their blood. Instead of all this, we have the homespun fates of Cephas and Prudence repeated in an infinite series of peaceable sameness, and finding space enough for record in the family Bible; we have the noise of axe and hammer and saw, an apotheosis of dogged work, where, reversing the fairy-tale, nothing is left to luck, and, if there be any poetry, it is something that cannot be helped,—the waste of the water over the dam. Extrinsically, it is prosaic and plebeian; intrinsically, it is poetic and noble; for it is, perhaps, the most perfect incarnation of an idea the world has ever seen. That idea was not to found a democracy, nor to charter the city of New Jerusalem by an act of the General Court, as gentlemen seem to think whose notions of history and human nature rise like an exhalation from the good things at a Pilgrim Society dinner. Not in the least. They had no faith in the Divine institution of a system which gives Teague, because he can dig, as much influence as Ralph, because he can think, nor in personal at the expense of general freedom. Their view of human rights was not so limited that it could not take in human relations and duties also. They would have been likely to answer the claim, "I am as good as anybody," by a quiet, "Yes, for some things, but not for others; as good, doubtless, in your place, where all things are good." What the early settlers of Massachusetts *did* intend, and what they accomplished, was the founding here of a *new* England, and a better one, where the political superstitions and abuses of the old should never have leave to take root. So much, we may say, they deliberately intended. No nobles, either lay or cleric, no great landed estates, and no universal ignorance as the seed-plot of vice and unreason; but an elective magistracy and clergy, land for all who would till it, and reading and writing, will ye nill ye, instead. Here at last, it would seem, simple manhood is to have a chance to play his stake against Fortune with honest dice, uncogged by those three hoary sharpers, Prerogative, Patricianism, and Priestcraft. Whoever has looked into the pamphlets published in England during the Great Rebellion cannot but have been struck by the fact, that the principles and practice of the Puritan colony had begun to react with considerable force on the mother country; and the policy of the retrograde party there, after the Restoration, in its dealings with New England, finds a curious parallel as to its motives (time will show whether as to its results) in the conduct of the same party towards America during the last four years.[2] This influence and this fear alike bear witness to the energy of the principles at work here.

We have said that the details of New England history were essentially dry and unpoetic. Everything is near, authentic, and petty. There is no mist of distance to soften outlines, no mirage of tradition to give characters and events an imaginative loom. So much downright work was perhaps never wrought on the earth's surface in the same space of time as during the first forty years after the settlement. But mere work is unpicturesque, and void of sentiment. Irving instinctively and admirably illustrated in his "Knickerbocker" the humorous element which lies in this nearness of view, this clear, prosaic daylight of modernness, and this poverty of stage-properties, which makes

[2] The years of the Civil War.—Ed.

the actors and the deeds they were concerned in seem ludicrously small when contrasted with the semi-mythic grandeur in which we have clothed them, looking backward from the crowned result, and fancying a cause as majestic as our conception of the effect. There was, indeed, one poetic side to the existence otherwise so narrow and practical; and to have conceived this, however partially, is the one original and American thing in Cooper. This diviner glimpse illumines the lives of our Daniel Boones, the man of civilization and old-world ideas confronted with our forest solitudes,—confronted, too, for the first time, with his real self, and so led gradually to disentangle the original substance of his manhood from the artificial results of culture. Here was our new Adam of the wilderness, forced to name anew, not the visible creation of God, but the invisible creation of man, in those forms that lie at the base of social institutions, so insensibly molding personal character and controlling individual action. Here is the protagonist of our New World epic, a figure as poetic as that of Achilles, as ideally representative as that of Don Quixote, as romantic in its relation to our homespun and plebeian mythus as Arthur in his to the mailed and plumed cycle of chivalry. We do not mean, of course, that Cooper's "Leatherstocking" is all this or anything like it, but that the character typified in him is ideally and potentially all this and more.

But whatever was poetical in the lives of the early New-Englanders had something shy, if not sombre, about it. If their natures flowered, it was out of sight, like the fern. It was in the practical that they showed their true quality, as Englishmen are wont. It has been the fashion lately with a few feeble-minded persons to undervalue the New-England Puritans, as if they were nothing more than gloomy and narrow-minded fanatics. But all the charges brought against these large-minded and far-seeing men are precisely those which a really able fanatic, Joseph de Maistre, lays at the door of Protestantism. Neither a knowledge of human nature nor of history justifies us in confounding, as is commonly done, the Puritans of Old and New England, or the English Puritans of the third with those of the fifth decade of the seventeenth century. Fanaticism, or, to call it by its milder name, enthusiasm, is only powerful and active so long as it is aggressive. Establish it firmly in power, and it becomes conservatism, whether it will or no. A sceptre once put in the hand, the grip is instinctive; and he who is firmly seated in authority soon learns to think security, and not progress, the highest lesson of statecraft. From the summit of power men no longer turn their eyes upward only, but begin to look about them. Aspiration sees only one side of every question; possession, many. And the English Puritans, after their revolution was accomplished, stood in even a more precarious position than most successful assailants of the prerogative of whatever *is* to continue in being. They had carried a political end by means of a religious revival. The fulcrum on which they rested their lever to overturn the existing order of things (as history always placidly calls the particular form of *dis*order for the time being) was in the soul of man. They could not renew the fiery gush of enthusiasm, when once the molten metal had begun to stiffen in the mold of policy and precedent. The religious element of Puritanism became insensibly merged in the political; and, its one great man taken away, it died, as passions have done before, of possession. It was one thing to shout with Cromwell before the battle of Dunbar, "Now, Lord, arise, and let thine enemies be scattered!" and to snuffle, "Rise, Lord, and keep us safe in our benefices, our sequestered estates, and our five per cent!" Puritanism meant something when Captain Hodgson, riding out to battle through the morning mist, turns over the command of his troop to a lieutenant, and stays to hear the prayer of a cornet, there was "so much of God in it." Become traditional, repeating the phrase without the spirit, reading the present backward as if it were written in Hebrew, translating Jehovah by "I was" instead of "I am,"—it was no more like its former self than the hollow drum made of Zisca's skin was like the grim captain whose soul it had once contained. Yet the change was inevitable, for it is not safe to confound the things of Cæsar with the things of God. Some honest republicans, like Ludlow, were never able to comprehend the chilling contrast between the ideal aim and the material fulfilment, and looked askance on the strenuous reign of Oliver,—that rugged boulder of primitive manhood lying lonely there on the dead level of the century,—as if some crooked changeling had been laid in the cradle instead of the fair babe of a Commonwealth they had dreamed. Truly there is a tide in the affairs of men, but there is no gulf-stream setting forever in one direction; and those waves of enthusiasm on whose crumbling crests we sometimes see nations lifted for a gleaming moment are wont to have a gloomy trough before and behind.

But the founders of New England, though they must have sympathized vividly with the struggles and triumphs of their brethren in the mother country, were never subjected to the same trials and temptations, never hampered with the same lumber of usages and tradition. They were not driven to win power by doubtful or desperate ways, nor to maintain it by any compromises of the ends which make it worth having. From the outset they were builders, without need of first pulling down, whether to make room or provide material. For thirty years after the colonization of the Bay, they had absolute power to mold as they would the character of their adolescent commonwealth. During this time a whole generation would have grown to manhood who knew the Old World only by report, in whose habitual thought kings, nobles, and bishops would be as far away from all present and practical concern as the figures in a fairy tale, and all whose memories and associations, all their unconscious training by eye and ear, were New English wholly. Nor were the men whose influence was greatest in shaping the framework and the policy of the Colony, in any true sense of the word, fanatics. Enthusiasts, perhaps, they were, but with them the fermentation had never gone further than the ripeness of the vinous stage. Disappointment had never made it acetous, nor had it ever putrefied into the turbid zeal of Fifth-Monarchism and sectarian whimsy. There is no better ballast for keeping the mind steady on its keel, and saving it from all risk of *crankiness,* than business. And they were business men, men of facts and figures no less than of religious earnestness. The sum of two hundred thousand pounds had been invested in their undertaking,—a sum, for that time, truly enormous as the result of private combination for a doubtful experiment. That their enterprise might succeed, they must show a balance on the right side of the counting-house ledger, as well as in their private accounts with their own souls. The liberty of praying when and how they would, must be balanced with an ability of paying when and as they ought. Nor is the resulting fact in this case at variance with the *a priori* theory. They succeeded in making their thought the life and soul of a body politic, still powerful, still benignly operative, after two centuries; a thing which no mere fanatic ever did or ever will accomplish. Sober, earnest, and thoughtful men, it was no Utopia, no New Atlantis, no realization of a splendid dream, which they had at heart, but the establishment of the divine principle of Authority on the common interest and the common consent; the making, by a contribution from the free-will of all, a power which should curb and guide the free-will of each for the general good. If they were stern in their dealings with sectaries, it should be remembered that the Colony was in fact the private property of the Massachusetts Company, that unity was essential to its success, and that John of Leyden had taught them how unendurable by the nostrils of honest men is the corruption of the right of private judgment in the evil and selfish hearts of men when no thorough mental training has developed the understanding and given the judgment its needful means of comparison and correction. They knew that liberty in the hands of feeble-minded and unreasoning persons (and all the worse if they are honest) means nothing more than the supremacy of their particular form of imbecility; means nothing less, therefore, than downright chaos, a Bedlam-chaos of monomaniacs and bores. What was to be done with men and women, who bore conclusive witness to the fall of man by insisting on walking up the broad-aisle of the meeting-house in a costume which that event had put forever out of fashion? About their treatment of witches, too, there has been a great deal of ignorant babble. Puritanism had nothing whatever to do with it. They acted under a delusion, which, with an exception here and there (and those mainly medical men, like Wierus and Webster), darkened the understanding of all Christendom. Dr. Henry More was no Puritan; and his letter to Glanvil, prefixed to the third edition of the "Sadducismus Triumphatus," was written in 1678, only fourteen years before the trials at Salem. Bekker's "Bezauberte Welt" was published in 1693; and in the Preface he speaks of the difficulty of overcoming "the prejudices in which not only ordinary men, but the learned also, are obstinate." In Hathaway's case, 1702, Chief Justice Holt, in charging the jury, expresses no disbelief in the possibility of witchcraft, and the indictment implies its existence. Indeed, the natural reaction from the Salem mania of 1692 put an end to belief in devilish compacts and demoniac possessions sooner in New England than elsewhere. The last we hear of it there is in 1720, when Rev. Mr. Turell of Medford detected and exposed an attempted cheat by two girls. Even in 1692, it was the foolish breath of Cotton Mather and others of the clergy that blew the dying embers of this ghastly superstition into a flame; and they were actuated partly by a desire to bring about a religious revival, which might stay for a while the hastening lapse of their own authority, and still more by that credulous scepticism of feeble-minded piety which dreads the cutting away of an orthodox misbelief, as if the life-blood of faith would follow, and would keep even a stumbling-block in the way of salvation, if only enough generations had tripped over it to make it venerable. The witches were condemned on precisely the same grounds that in our day led to the condemnation of "Essays and Reviews."

But Puritanism was already in the decline when such things were possible. What had been a wondrous and intimate experience of the soul, a flash into the very crypt and basis of man's nature from the fire of trial, had become ritual and tradition. In prosperous times the faith of one generation becomes the formality of the next. "The necessity of a reformation," set forth by order of the Synod which met at Cambridge in 1679, though no doubt overstating the case, shows how much even at that time the ancient strictness had been loosened. The country had grown rich, its commerce was large, and wealth did its natural work in making life softer and more worldly, commerce in deprovincializing the minds of those engaged in it. But Puritanism had already done its duty. As there are certain creatures whose whole being seems occupied with an egg-laying errand they are sent upon, incarnate ovipositors, their bodies but bags to hold this precious deposit, their legs of use only to carry them where they may safeliest be rid of it, so sometimes a generation seems to have no other end than the conception and ripening of certain germs. Its blind stirrings, its apparently aimless seeking hither and thither, are but the driving of an instinct to be done with its parturient function toward these principles of future life and power. Puritanism, believing itself quick with the seed of religious liberty, laid, without knowing it, the egg of democracy. The English Puritans pulled down church and state to rebuild Zion on the ruins, and all the while it was not Zion, but America, they were building. But if their millennium went by, like the rest, and left men still human,—if they, like so many saints and martyrs before them, listened in vain for the sound of that trumpet which was to summon all souls to a resurrection from the body of this death which men call life,—it is not for us, at least, to forget the heavy debt we owe them. It was the drums of Naseby and Dunbar that gathered the minute-men on Lexington Common; it was the red dint of the axe on Charles's block that marked One in our era. The Puritans had their faults. They were narrow, ungenial; they could not understand the text, "I have piped to you and ye have not danced," nor conceive that saving one's soul should be the cheerfullest, and not the dreariest of businesses. Their preachers had a way, like the painful Mr. Perkins, of pronouncing the word *damn* with such an emphasis as left a doleful echo in their auditors' ears a good while after. And it was natural that men who had led or accompanied the exodus from existing forms and associations into the doubtful wilderness that led to the promised land, should find more to their purpose in the Old Testament than in the New. As respects the New England settlers, however visionary some of their religious tenets may have been, their political ideas savored of the realty, and it was no Nephelococcygia of which they drew the plan, but of a commonwealth whose foundation was to rest on solid and familiar earth. If what they did was done in a corner, the results of it were to be felt to the ends of the earth; and the figure of Winthrop should be as venerable in history as that of Romulus is barbarously grand in legend.

We are inclined to think that many of our national characteristics, which are sometimes attributed to climate and sometimes to institutions, are traceable to the influences of Puritan descent. We are apt to forget how very large a proportion of our population is descended from emigrants who came over before 1660. Those emigrants were in great part representatives of that element of English character which was most susceptible of religious impressions; in other words, the most earnest and imaginative. Our people still differ from their English cousins (as they are fond of calling themselves when they are afraid we may do them a mischief) in a certain capacity for enthusiasm, a devotion to abstract principle, an openness to ideas, a greater aptness for intuitions than for the slow processes of the syllogism, and, as derivative from this, in minds of looser texture, a light-armed, skirmishing habit of thought, and a positive preference of the birds in the bush,—an excellent quality of character *before* you have your bird in the hand.

There have been two great distributing centres of the English race on this continent, Massachusetts and Virginia. Each has impressed the character of its early legislators on the swarms it has sent forth. Their ideas are in some fundamental respects the opposites of each other, and we can only account for it by an antagonism of thought beginning with the early framers of their respective institutions. New England abolishes caste; in Virginia they still talk of "quality folks." But it was in making education not only common to all, but in some sense compulsory on all, that the destiny of the free republics of America was practically settled. Every man was to be trained, not only to the use of arms, but of his wits also; and it is these which alone make the others effective weapons for the maintenance of freedom. You may disarm the hands, but not the brains, of a people, and to know what should be defended is the first condition of successful defense. Simple as it seems, it was a great discovery that the key of knowledge could turn both ways, that it could open, as well as lock, the door of power to the many. The only things a New Englander was ever locked out of were the jails. It is quite true that our Republic is the heir of the English Commonwealth; but as we trace events backward to their causes, we shall find it true also, that what made our Revolution a foregone conclusion was that act of the General Court, passed in May, 1647, which established the system of common schools. "To the end that learning may not be buried in the graves of our forefathers in Church and Commonwealth, the Lord assisting our endeavors, it is therefore ordered by this Court and authority thereof, that every township in this jurisdiction, after the Lord hath increased them to fifty householders, shall then forthwith appoint one within their own towns to teach all such children as shall resort to him to write and read."

Passing through some Massachusetts village, perhaps at a distance from any house, it may be in the midst of a piece of woods where four roads meet, one may sometimes even yet see a small, square, one-story building, whose use would not be long doubtful. It is summer, and the flickering shadows of forest-leaves dapple the roof of the little porch, whose door stands wide, and shows, hanging on either hand, rows of straw hats and bonnets, that look as if they had done good service. As you pass the open windows, you hear whole platoons of high-pitched voices discharging words of two or three syllables with wonderful precision and unanimity. Then there is a pause, and the voice of the officer in command is heard reproving some raw recruit whose vocal musket hung fire. Then the drill of the small infantry begins anew, but pauses again because some urchin—who agrees with Voltaire that the superfluous is a very necessary thing—insists on spelling "subtraction" with an *s* too much.

If you had the good fortune to be born and bred in the Bay State, your mind is thronged with half-sad, half-humorous recollections. The a-b abs of little voices long since hushed in the mold, or ringing now in the pulpit, at the bar, or in the Senate-chamber, come back to the ear of memory. You remember the high stool on which culprits used to be elevated with the tall paper fool's-cap on their heads, blushing to the ears; and you think with wonder how you have seen them since as men climbing the world's penance-stools of ambition without a blush, and gladly giving everything for life's caps and bells. And you have pleasanter memories of going after pond-lilies, of angling for horn-pouts,—that queer bat among the fishes,—of nutting, of walking over the creaking snow-crust in winter, when the warm breath of every household was curling up silently in the keen blue air. You wonder if life has any rewards more solid and permanent than the Spanish dollar that was hung around your neck to be restored again next day, and conclude sadly that it was but too true a prophecy and emblem of all worldly success. But your moralizing is broken short off by a rattle of feet and the pouring forth of the whole swarm,—the boys dancing and shouting,—the mere effervescence of the fixed air of youth and animal spirits uncorked,—the sedater girls in confidential twos and threes decanting secrets out of the mouth of one cape-bonnet into that of another. Times have changed since the jackets and trousers used to draw up on one side of the road, and the petticoats on the other, to salute with bow and courtesy the white neckcloth of the parson or the squire, if it chanced to pass during intermission.

Now this little building, and others like it, were an original kind of fortification invented by the founders of New England. They are the martello-towers that protect our coast. This was the great discovery of our Puritan forefathers. They were the first lawgivers who saw clearly and enforced practically the simple moral and political truth, that knowledge was not an alms to be dependent on the chance charity of private men or the precarious pittance of a trust-fund, but a sacred debt which the commonwealth owed to every one of her children. The opening of the first grammar-school was the opening of the first trench against monopoly in church and state; the first row of trammels and pothooks which the little Shearjashubs and Elkanahs blotted and blubbered across their copy-books, was the preamble to the Declaration of Independence. The men who gave every man the chance to become a landholder, who made the transfer of land easy, and put knowledge within the reach of all, have been called narrow-minded, because they were intolerant. But intolerant of what? Of what they believed to be dangerous nonsense, which, if left free, would destroy the last hope of civil and religious freedom. They had not come here that every man might do that which seemed good in his own eyes, but in the sight of God. Toleration, moreover, is something which is won, not granted. It is the equilibrium of neutralized forces. The Puritans had no notion of tolerating mischief. They looked upon their little commonwealth as upon their own private estate and homestead, as they had a right to do, and would no more allow the Devil's religion of unreason to be preached therein, than we should permit a prize-fight in our gardens. They were narrow; in other words, they had an edge to them, as men that serve in great emergencies must; for a Gordian knot is settled sooner with a sword than a beetle. Nothing can be better than Dr. Palfrey's treatment of this question in the cases of Mr. Williams and

Mrs. Hutchinson. It is perfectly fair, and yet immitigable, as common-sense always is.

Having already had occasion to speak of Dr. Palfrey in our journal,[3] we have here done little more than epitomize the thoughts and conclusions to which we have been led, or in which we have been confirmed, by the three volumes already published. There are many passages which we should have been glad to quote; but it is to the praise of his work that its merit lies more in its tone of thought and its weight of opinion, than in pictorial effects. Brilliancy is cheap, but trustworthiness of thought, and evenness of judgment, are not to be had at every booth.

Dr. Palfrey combines in the temper of his mind and the variety of his experience some quite peculiar qualifications for the task he has undertaken. A man of singular honesty of purpose and conscientiousness of action, a thoroughly trained theologian, he ripened and enlarged the somewhat partial knowledge of mankind and their motives which falls to the lot of a clergyman by the experience of active politics and the training of practical statesmanship. Needing office neither as an addition of emolument nor of dignity, his interest in politics was the result of moral convictions, and not of personal ambition. The loss of his seat in Congress, while it was none to himself, was an irreparable one for Massachusetts, to which his integrity, his learning, and his eloquence were at once a service and an honor. In

[3] The North American Review.—Ed.

the maturity of his powers, he devoted himself to the composition of the History which he has now brought to the end of its third volume, and to the beginning of a new period. It is little to say that his work is the only one of its kind. He has done it so well, that it is likely to remain so. With none of that glitter of style and epigrammatic point of expression which please more than they enlighten, and tickle when they should instruct, there is a gravity and precision of thought, a sober dignity of expression, an equanimity of judgment, and a clear apprehension of characters and events, which give us the very truth of things as they are, and not as either he or his reader might wish them to be. Moreover, in spite of a certain external incongruity, incidental to the nature of the subject, which obliges him to go from one Colony to another, but which is more apparent than real, there is an essential unity of treatment, such as would be possible only for one who, knowing the facts thoroughly, had weighed and compared them well, and had thus been able to arrive at that neutral point of criticism which harmonizes by combining them all.

Here, it seems to us, lies the originality of Dr. Palfrey's work,—in this congruity of the controlling idea with the admitted event, without violence to either. The historian has his theory and his facts, and the only way in which he can reconcile them with each other is by bearing constantly in mind the human nature of the actors. In this instance there is no temptation to make a hero, who shall sum up in his own individuality and carry forward by his own will that purpose of which we seem to catch such bewildering glances in history, which reveals itself more clearly and constantly, perhaps, in the annals of New England than elsewhere, and which yet, at best, is but tentative, doubtful of itself, turned this way and that by chance, made up of instinct, and modified by circumstance quite as much as it is directed by deliberate forethought. Such a purpose, or natural craving, or result of temporary influences, may be misguided by a powerful character to his own ends, or, if he be strongly in sympathy with it, may be hastened toward its own fulfilment; but there is no such heroic element in our drama, and what is remarkable is, that, under whatever government, democracy grew with the growth of the New England Colonies, and was at last potent enough to wrench them, and the better part of the continent with them, from the mother country. It is true that Jefferson embodied in the Declaration of Independence the speculative theories he had learned in France, but the impulse to separation came from Massachusetts; and the theories had long since been embodied there in the practice of the people, if they had never been formulated in distinct propositions.

We do not mean that Dr. Palfrey, like a great many declaimers about the Pilgrim Fathers, looks upon them all as men of grand conceptions and superhuman foresight. An entire ship's company of Columbuses is what the world never saw. Nor has he formed any theory and fitted his facts to it, as a man in a hurry is apt to cram his traveling-bag, with a total disregard of shape or texture. But he has found that the facts will only fit comfortably together on a single plan, namely, that the fathers did have a conception (which those will call grand who regard simplicity as a necessary element of grandeur) of founding here a commonwealth on those two eternal bases of Faith and Work; that they had, indeed, no revolutionary ideas of universal liberty, but yet, what answered the purpose quite as well, an abiding faith in the brotherhood of men as children of God; and that they did not so much propose to make all things new, as to develop the latent possibilities of English law and English character, by clearing away the fences by which the abuse of the one was gradually discommoning the other from the broad fields of natural right. They were not in advance of their age, as it is called, for no one who is so can ever work profitably in it; but they were alive to the highest and most earnest thinking of their time. Dr. Palfrey also makes it clear that the thought of separation from the parent state was not only not unfamiliar to the minds of the leaders of New England emigration, but that they looked forward to it and prepared for it as something that might be expedient or necessary according to the turn of events. Apart from contemporary evidence of their hopes and intentions, he finds in the inevitable results of the institutions they founded the proof of what they meant to do.

The present volume brings the history down to one of the limits which the author had originally set to his labors,—the fall of the Andros government. He tells the story of King Philip's war with satisfactory minuteness, quoting the picturesque passages of earlier narrators; he gives us a most interesting and instructive chapter on the early legislation of the Colonies, useful for the final extinction of some old falsehoods, which still give a buzz now and then, like winter flies; and he traces the gradual decline, we will not say of the public spirit, but in the moral courage and principle of those who should have been its inspirers and leaders. We are come now upon a new generation, prosperous in their affairs, and forgetful alike of the trials of the pioneers and of the end for which they thought it light to endure them. The day of compromises and expedients had arrived. This is not the first time in the course of his history that Dr. Palfrey, by his interpretation and comment of the past, has given a new meaning to events that have taken place under our own eyes; and we suspect that it was by no mere study of contemporary documents that he learned how to appreciate the motives of the men to whom they relate. There is an admirable consistency and candor in his portraits of the leaders of this period of decline; and the reproof of timidity and self-seeking is not unbecoming in the mouth of one who has himself made sacrifices for principle, and never flinched in the service of truth.

In the Preface, Dr. Palfrey bids farewell to his work with an affectionate regret that has something almost pathetic in it. In spite of his farewell speech, however, and the falling of the curtain, we cannot help hoping that he will greet us again in successive last appearances, till he has brought his work down to the end of another of those cycles of which he speaks.

"But the cycle of New England is eighty-six years. In the spring of 1603, the family of Stuart ascended the throne of England. At the end of eighty-six years, Massachusetts having been betrayed to her enemies by her most eminent and trusted citizen, Joseph Dudley, the people, on the 19th day of April, 1689, committed their prisoner, the deputy of the Stuart King, to the fort in Boston which he had built to overawe them. Another eighty-six years passed, and Massachusetts had been betrayed to her enemies by her most eminent and trusted citizen, Thomas Hutchinson, when, at Lexington and Concord, on the 19th of April, 1775, her farmers struck the first blow in the War of American Independence. Another eighty-six years ensued, and a domination of slaveholders, more odious than that of Stuarts or of Guelphs, had been fastened upon her, when, on the 19th of April, 1861, the streets of Baltimore were stained by the blood of her soldiers on their way to uphold liberty and law by the rescue of the National Capital."

In taking leave of Dr. Palfrey, then, as we prefer to say, for the present, we cannot but congratulate him on the real service he has done to our history, and to the understanding of our national character. Patient, thoughtful, exact, and with those sensitive moral sympathies which are worth more than all else to an historian, he has added to our stock of truth, and helped us in the way of right thinking. No doubt there are periods and topics more picturesque, but we think him most sure of lasting fame who has chosen a subject where the deepest interest is a moral one; for while men weary of pictures, there is always that in the deep things of God which sooner or later attracts and charms them.